T3-BGM-779

Contents

Preface

Designing Restaurant Interiors is a restaurant owner's guide to the successful handling of the design of restaurant interiors. A wall-to-wall, floor-to-ceiling story, *Designing Restaurant Interiors* is useful to both new investors and current owners, helping to solve the design problems related to the front end of the restaurant—all that meets the customer's eye from the time of his arrival, through his dining experience, until his departure.

Whether or not to be your own designer, how to approach a remodeling job, how to select a restaurant theme, how to remedy structural defects, how to use color effectively are among the decisions—faced by you from the beginning of your investment—that are covered in the text. Much of the text, fully illustrated to demonstrate relevant points, is geared toward giving you a sense of how particular restaurant themes can be developed through interior design. In addition, *Designing Restaurant Interiors* provide insights into working with designers and coordinating designer-architect teams.

The thrust of the text is to provide an overview of the interior design experience in order to help you plan your design investment wisely and effectively.

Chapter 1

Do You Need a Designer?

Everyone knows a Jack-of-all-trades; he is the person who does anything and everything—equally unsuccessfully. In the past, there were many such people in the restaurant business. To open a new restaurant years ago, you might buy a stove, a sink, a lunch counter, stools, tables, chairs, and a few fixtures to light the interior. Then you would paint the restaurant a not undesirable color, find a cook, hang up a sign that advertised "Restaurant," and open the doors. The restaurant's only competition then was another restaurant that was begun in the same manner. It was reasonable to assume that you could compete with another operator with no better skills than yours.

This was at a time when the restaurateur had more of a captive trade. The people in the neighborhood would walk to the restaurant instead of driving to another location. Once driving became more popular, however, customers could be more choosy about the restaurants they frequented. They could go farther to select a place to eat. Thus the fellow with the simple, informal approach was put to the test to keep his trade.

WHEN TO CONSIDER A DESIGNER

And people did drive farther. With the improvement of the automobile and the highways and with the increase in adequate parking lots, restaurant customers became more selective. They could afford to bypass the places they formerly walked to and drive to a choicer place.

When customers become more mobile, the restaurant owner is forced to make improvements in his operation. He might improve the quality of the food, the size and character of the sign, or the exterior of the building. Our concern here is with improvement in the quality of the interior—that portion of the investment that begins at the front door, ends at the exit, and covers all the areas within the customer's domain, from wall to wall and from floor to ceiling. It is in this public area that the diner's impressions of the total investment are created. It is in this area that the owner may add to the comfort or discomfort of the diner—a factor which has a definite bearing on the number of times the diner may be counted on to return. It is in this area that the quality of decisions has a heavy influence on future profits.

But who is to design the hoped-for improvements in the interior? Aren't we all interior designers at one time or another? The question for the restaurant investor is whether or not he shall continue to be his own designer.

THE OWNER AS DESIGNER

The problem of the design of the interior of a restaurant is that it requires the study of products and services involved in many different fields. It therefore calls for coordination of the decision making in these many, and otherwise unrelated, fields. The owner is not the best designer of his own interior because he already has "too many hats to wear." First, he is the dreamer, the overall planner, the promoter, the financier, and the manager who has to put the total package together in the beginning. Then, he is the person who does the hiring and firing, who determines the quality of the supplies to be purchased, and who selects the type of recipes to be prepared. He decides on the size of the restaurant; the number of persons he wants to serve; the selection of the site; and the training of the chef, waitresses, and other help. He is the person who determines the advertising campaign and purchases it. He is the general purchasing agent for all things, the public relations person, and, last but not least, the host himself.

If he were master of as many as a half dozen of these skills, he might be a success without really being expert in the rest. So often, however, a man or woman who is a good cook will open a restaurant and hope that all other things will fall in line. So often, also, a person who is a good salesman will similarly invest in a restaurant, hoping that he can sell whatever type of food he happens to come up with to whomever his potential customers might be. Then, there is the person who may be a successful money manager who hopes to be efficient in handling all other phases of the operation of a restaurant. There is seldom a master of all trades—a person who needs no help in any of the many phases of the work in a restaurant investment.

DEALERS OF SPECIALTY PRODUCTS

Thumbing through the Yellow Pages of his local phone book, the restaurant owner will find many firms who advertise free decorator services. These ads for free interior decorating are offered as inducements to buy a multitude of products, such as paint, wallpaper, drapery fabrics, carpeting, light fixtures, acoustical tile ceiling materials, wood wall panels, and art work. One limitation is evident. If the free services of the sellers of specialty products are used, there is little opportunity to secure competitive pricing for the purchase of the particular specialty of the house making the free offer. The restaurateur is obligated to deal with the specialty house for those products that it offers to sell. Another limitation is that the interior designer for a firm that deals in a single line of specific products tends to concentrate only on that particular line.

CHINA AND GLASSWARE DEALERS

Interior decorating services are also offered by many of the china and glassware dealers. Such firms hope that they will obligate the restaurant operator to buy their kitchen supplies, china, glassware, chairs, tables, booths, carpeting, and draperies, in one complete package. The quality of these all-in-one package deals, which include everything but the selection of the chef, must be carefully weighed by the restaurant owner. The owner must be sure that the firm he chooses does not fall into the Jack-of-all-trades-master-of-none category.

If the firms have trained specialists in kitchen layout apart from those who are trained in the designing of the customer's area, the owner may look to them as an acceptable purchasing source. In many instances, however, the china and glassware dealers who label themselves "restaurant outfitters" or "complete restaurant furnishers" are the single enfranchised dealers for certain product manufacturers. In order to hold on to the franchise, the dealer habitually specifies his franchised line in the design of the restaurant. The result is a lack of competition when it comes to the purchase of the product itself. The dealer is in a position, as the interior designer, to work into the interior certain features, patterns, and colors that demand the purchase of his own enfranchised line. The cost to the owner is the right to get competitive quotations.

Only if the owner pays for interior design services is the specification of a predetermined product or line of goods avoided. The owner is only in a position to secure competitive bids if the products are selected from what is known as "open lines."

ARCHITECTS

In the case of building new restaurant buildings as against the remodeling of older properties, the architect may naturally have the first chance to at least shape the interior spaces—that is, to determine the size and shape of the spaces themselves. It is up to the owner how much the architect controls the design of the interior.

When designing a new building on an open lot, the architect, without input from the owner or from others, ordinarily decides the size and shape of all spaces within the structure. Only the selection of the furnishings is left to the owner or an interior designer. Many good restaurants have been designed through all phases by the architect. Where the complete interiors are also designed by the architect, it is important that there be a person on the architect's staff who specializes in interior furniture and furnishings. Otherwise, the rigidity of the "engineer" in the architect may show up in the finished product—a restaurant that passes the community building codes, but does not excite potential customers.

FREE-LANCE INTERIOR DESIGNERS

Whether building a new structure or remodeling an older property, the owner has the choice of securing the services of a professional, free-lance interior designer. On a new building, the professional interior designer can work cooperatively with the architect or engineer and with the owner. In the remodeling of an older property, the professional interior designer can handle the entire problem, working only with the owner.

Under the heading of professional interior designers, there are those who are free-lance, those who are connected with product manufacturers, and those connected with architects. Designers may be further divided into those who belong to accredited societies and those who do not. Formerly, there were three such societies: the American Institute of Interior Designers, which allowed the professional to attach the initials *A.I.D.* to his name; the National Society of Interior Designers, whose members used the initials *N.S.I.D.*; and the Interiors for Business Designers, whose members used the initials *I.B.D.*

Just as there are many architects who do not carry the initials *A.I.A.*, there are many professional interior designers who do not bear the initials after their names. Recently, the members of A.I.D. and N.S.I.D. joined hands to form the new American Society of Interior Designers with the initials *A.S.I.D.* So, at this moment, there are two societies of professional interior designers who publicly claim the highest standards of practice for this profession.

The designers who have been accredited by these two societies have undergone rigid testing to assure the public of a best performance in their fields. Most new members of A.S.I.D., for example, must have four years of college courses that are approved for interior designers plus at least one year of experience in the field before they are considered for testing for the right to eventually use the initials *A.S.I.D.* after their names. This is of benefit to the public. It is a safety measure that assures a potential buyer of obtaining skilled counsel. Once a restaurant investor has determined that he will employ a skilled interior designer, he should look for those whose names are followed by these initials in the same way, or by the same reasoning, that when he has a medical problem he seeks a person whose name carries the initials *M.D.*

WORKING WITH A DESIGNER-ARCHITECT TEAM

In the case of new buildings, the owner must decide who to call in first—the architect or the interior designer. Since the first concern of the designer will be the decision as to sizes and shapes of the spaces within the structure, it is a good idea for the designer to get the first call. In addition, the designer should be employed by the owner. He should not be subservient to the architect, but paid directly by the owner. In that way he can safely and fully express his design to a single employer. The designer then becomes a coworker with the architect, answering directly to the owner but cooperating with the architectural office.

Remember that while the customers will look at the building for less than a minute as they approach the building, they may spend half an hour to two hours or more in the interior. It simply stands to reason that the most important decisions concerning interior design be placed in the hands of the person who is most skilled in that area—the professional interior designer. This is not meant to deny credit to the architect who designs the structure and whose work is seen first by the potential customer. Rather, we mean simply to compare values and establish priorities. If the customer is happily entertained by the general appearance of the exterior for the minute it takes him to approach the building and is less than well pleased for the average forty-five minutes that he spends within, he probably will not return. Conversely, if he is not sufficiently attracted to enter the building in the first place, he will never get to enjoy the interior, even if it has been handled most successfully.

If the building is a new one, the best procedure is for the owner to select an interior designer and an architect (perhaps in that order) to work directly with him. He should let it be known from the beginning that while cooperation between them is desirable, neither one is to be subservient to the other. Neither the architect nor the professional interior designer needs to apologize to the other for expressing points on which he needs the cooperation of the other. In this way, a good team is formed, and the best result may be expected.

So, when starting a new or remodeling an old property for restaurant use, the owner has several options for handling the design of the interior spaces. The design can be accomplished by the owner himself, the free interior decorators offered by the paint and wallpaper houses, the decorators or designers or engineers offered by the china and glass-ware houses, the architect, or the professional interior designer of restaurants.

THE ILLUSION OF COST-FREE DESIGN

Let's now look at the final cost of the total restaurant investment in terms of how the choice of an interior designer reflects itself in this total figure. The owner who uses himself as the designer of the interiors is probably not a draftsman. He will therefore do the designing in a haphazard way as he goes along—buying dozen lots of various items in simple colors and patterns, just as things strike his fancy. There is little relationship between the purchase of one product and the purchase of another when purchases are made without a total plan in mind. Let's not, however, charge any cost factor or percentage figure here to the total investment, assuming that the owner will do this sort of decision making after hours, late at night, or on holidays. He may simply "throw it in" while determining and managing all the other factors involved in going into the restaurant business. It is easy to see that this is the cheapest way to design an interior. The cost, however, cannot be counted until years later when the result has been attended by either success or failure of the enterprise.

Temporarily, at least, there is no cost connected with the free decorator services offered by paint and wallpaper stores and other sellers of products that the operator will have to buy. The product seller, in these cases, does not actually give the service free; he merely adds it to the final selling price. Then, once the buyer has approved of the interior designs provided to him free, he is faced with a purchase price that carries the cost of the decorator services offered to him "without cost." He does not discover until a year or more later what the true value of the so-called free design advice has been.

This method of judging values applies to an even greater degree to the design services of a china and glassware house that offers to sell everything in the customers' area and everything in the kitchen (even to the walk-in cold storage boxes). Here, if the restaurant operator accepts the design services without charge, he surely feels obligated to deal for the total package with the supply house that provides his free interior designer. When a total package design is offered, and especially when it is offered free, the restaurateur often finds it not only embarrassing but difficult to buy any one or more of the products from a competitive source. The original firm will have successfully tied together and coordinated within the design the need for every one of their products—products for which they may even be singly enfranchised to the exclusion of competition from other firms.

In this case, you purchase the entire package when you agree to accept the free design. On the other hand, if the owner agrees to secure his interior design plans by purchasing them, it is not embarrassing, difficult, or out of line for him to submit the plans so prepared to other houses for competitive pricing.

In order to offer its design services free, the china and glassware merchant, or total package restaurant supply house, has to add a percentage on to purchases to cover these costs. We can estimate that in order to continue to give free design services and support a department of interior designers, the supply house has to set aside at least 10 percent of the total sale for each job that they design. Then we can estimate that the supply house may get only one contract out of every three jobs that it designs. You can quickly see how this affects the fellow who is the one of the three who buys. This original 10 percent, as well as 20 percent for the other two buyers to whom the supply house was not successful in selling, may be concealed in the total selling price.

So, as a supply house offers free design services to all takers, the ones who eventually buy the total package are paying not only for the designing of their own contract, but also for the services that the supply house offered to those who didn't buy. This represents a dangerous gamble for the supply house. They can only recover when they sell a package deal to the restaurant investor who accepts their free interior design services.

If you purchase the design services of a product seller or restaurant supply house, you may be given the choice of a number of ways to pay. Often, you can pay a percentage of the purchases specified; sometimes it is on an hourly basis. You can also pay on an hourly basis with a top figure based on a percentage of the purchases specified. Usually, there is sufficient deposit of "earnest money" to assure you the prompt and complete attention of the designer. The balance is paid upon final delivery of the lists of requirements plus the drawings and specifications. Some houses offer to apply these payments toward the purchases of the products, reducing the amount of the final bill by the amount that has already been paid for the design services.

JUDGING THE ARCHITECT'S FEE

When you extend an architect's contract to include the designing of the customers' areas of the interior as well, the architect must charge for this added service, if he is to do it well and properly. The charge may be on a flat fee basis for the design of the total package. Alternately, it is a percentage of the total purchases including the furnishings. A third method is to charge on a straight time basis where you are charged by the hour for these additional services. In any event, he will not make it a free gift. You can determine the amount you are paying the architect for interior design services: ask him to separate the charges for designing the building structure from the charges for designing the customers' areas regardless of which method of charging he employs.

Keep in mind that when an architect in speaking of a percentage of the total building cost raises this cost by a very small added percentage to include the interior designing, he is probably referring to a percentage of the *total cost of the building* (including furnishings), as compared with the cost of furnishings alone. Because of this difference in the amounts against which the percentage is counted, his very small additional percentage for including interior designs may look like much less than that charged by sellers of products or by free-lance, professional interior designers. The latter base their charges on the purchases of products rather than the purchase of the building.

The best way to get a comparative figure from the architect is to ask him for (1) a flat figure for the interior designs alone and separate from the building, (2) hourly charges alone and separate from charges for the design of the building, or (3) a percentage based on the total purchases of products for the interiors rather than on the cost of the total building.

HOW MUCH WILL A FREE-LANCE DESIGNER CHARGE?

Professional designers of the interiors, whether they are members of A.S.I.D. or of I.B.D. or are without society affiliation, work in several ways. They may charge you a flat fee, a percentage of the total product purchases specified by their office, or by the hour. They will also probably ask for an early retainer or fee to act as earnest money. You may expect to pay anywhere from 8 to 15 percent of your total furnishings purchases for the advice of a skilled interior designer for restaurants. If you opt to go with the professional interior designer or firm of designers, you may ask in your area which person or firm is the most experienced in designing the type of restaurant you want to operate—whether it be a small fast food type or a larger full-service operation. Then, if you select the designer that is best recommended for that field in which you wish to operate, you may expect specific values in return.

A prime value is in the selection of a firm that is not limited by franchise to promote the sale of a particular line of furniture or equipment. It is in this area that a large dollar value is lost, as a result of the lack of competition. At the drawing-board level, a professional interior designer for restaurants has the ability to select equipment and furnishings from a very wide range of sources. A good, competitive price for each of the hundreds of items to be purchased is not obtained through the designer's allegiance to one particular manufacturer over another, but rather by his ability and willingness to research the best purchase for every item that you will need. You will not have made the best purchases if your designer has not made a careful and widespread search among many catalog sources to assure you of the best buy for each item.

It is here that we should mention the quality of the product that the buyer secures for his dollar. Often we hear buyers speak of the prices only and not in terms of the quality of the products that they secure. It is easy to tally the number of dollars that are spent, but it is not very easy to describe the quality *for which* the dollars were spent. The language to describe the quality of a product is more complicated; it comes from a thorough knowledge of the quality of many similar products from which the selections were finally made. The professional interior designer is fully equipped to judge quality. In addition, he should not be prejudiced in favor of a manufacturer except for reasons of cost and quality.

A shipment of chairs many of which break up during the first six months of use should be carefully evaluated against a shipment of chairs that last for twenty to thirty years without trouble. These considerations make the difference between a purchase being worth only 10 percent of the price you pay or 100 percent. So, as a buyer, think not only of the number of dollars which you are paying for an item, but also about the quality you are buying. Otherwise, you may receive only 10 percent of the value for which you are paying 100 percent in dollars. Don't be misguided by surface savings of only 5 or 10 percent.

The properly equipped office of a professional interior designer for restaurants should have a library consisting of thousands of catalogs beyond and including the Sweet's files normally found in the architect's office. A wide variety of fabric, carpeting, and wall covering samples should be found in a well-kept and up-to-the-minute library. The interior designer should have fingertip control of all suppliers of the products he specifies. He should know the market thoroughly in terms of price and quality.

PROS AND CONS

Looking backward over those who may handle the problem of designing the interior spaces for the restaurant, we see certain considerations emerge. If the owner uses himself as the designer, he must first decide whether that is the work in which he is most capable. He should keep in mind his competitors' freedom to choose to use specialists in this area. When he considers the use of free interior decorators who are offered in order to help sell products, he should first decide whether he wants to limit the competition on his purchases to the place whose decorator services he has accepted.

Then, as he looks upon the interior decorators or designers of the china and glassware houses, he should ask himself whether he wants to obligate himself for the purchase of furniture, furnishings, china, glassware, kitchen equipment, pots, kettles, and silverware as a result of his selection of the interior design services offered by these firms. Similarly, he must consider, in choosing an architect, which of the available architects is more an engineer and which is more a creative designer. He may even locate an architect with a department that concerns itself entirely with the design of the interior. He also has the option of choosing an architect who specializes in the design of restaurants, both inside and out. The owner's selection must then be compared with the employment of a professional interior designer, preferably one who is free-lance—and still more to be preferred, one who specializes in interior designs for restaurants.

In summary, you may find that little of real value is offered for free. And when something of sizable value is offered without visible charge, you must determine just how and where you are paying for it. Then decide whether you want your hands to be tied in this manner; that is, by accepting a free gift with the realization that the payment for it eventually will be found in the price tag.

Chapter 2

Can You Design It Yourself?

The restaurant owner who rents a space with a simple front, and whose desire to be an interior designer equals his interest in making profits, may decide to enter upon an adventure in restaurant design. If his storefront space is in a highly populated area, it is likely to secure enough traffic to operate in the black. Moreover, if parking space is insufficient to lure customers from any significant distance, the interior design of the restaurant may never need to be superior. The restaurant, regardless of interior design, can simply rely on its proximity to a maximum number of potential customers to guarantee a reasonable daily volume. Nevertheless, the owner is taking a big chance.

Whenever we compare the interior designs of competing restaurants, we must assume that all other things are equal: that is, that there is equality in the choice of a practical location, ease of access to the interior, quality of the overall management, character and experience of the personnel, quality of the food and service, and price range.

Even in a situation where restaurant parking is limited so that the owner must rely upon the people who are captive to his location, there is still the possibility that another restaurant may be opened in the immediate vicinity. Then begins the fight for life. If the owner counted heavily on having a captive trade and felt that the lack of parking space discouraged customers from other areas, he probably discounted the need for advice from a professional interior designer or an architect and handled the complete furnishing of the interior on his own.

It is when competition moves in a door or two away that his success is put to test. For now he discovers that by neglecting to employ the best of counsel in the design of his interior, he has failed to secure the favored place in the hearts of his customers. If competition moves in soon after he establishes himself, it may be too late to save the original investment in the interior furnishings. Even if he hasn't already invested his last expendable dollar in the original furnishings program, it will still be too soon to redecorate—regardless of the threat of the competitor. This will be the moment of truth. He will have to question the wisdom of being both restaurant owner and interior designer at the same time.

SELECTING A NAME

Let's retrace the preferences, selections, and decisions that a typical design-your-own restaurant owner will make as he takes on the job of both restaurant operator and interior designer.

We might begin with the selection of a name. It is only customary to expect the name to indicate something of what the diner will experience when visiting a new restaurant. The name may indicate the type of product that is served; for example, at Burger Chef, we expect to be served hamburgers. It might describe the speed of the service; the name "Minute Chef" gives us a clue to speedy service. We know that in a cafeteria we will stand in line and select food directly from the main supply containers. When we see a name like "Romano," we expect to eat spaghetti. "Antoine's" indicates French cuisine. And "Buccaneer" refers to an atmosphere reminiscent of pirates. The job of the owner/designer is to choose a name that fits the products, type of service, style of preparation, and type of decor that applies in each case, or one that has other values that may outweigh these. The owner would do well, in making his selection, to tentatively line up a dozen or more names for consideration and not make a final decision until he begins to think about what he is capable of doing to carry out the intent and meaning of the name selected.

Even after the name is selected, there are hundreds of printer's typefaces and lettering styles to be considered in determining the style of signs, menus, billboards, and advertising.

In order to choose the best name and the best printer's type and style in which to present the name, the owner will find himself having to determine the style of the furnishings and the interiors. All elements must relate to one another; the main theme should be carried through the name selection, style of presentation, and character of the interior.

FIRST THINGS FIRST

If the owner delays these decisions until the various elements more closely relate and cooperate with each other, he will find that he must add a few more areas of choice to the growing list of possibilities. For example, there will be the need to determine the size and shape and style of the chinaware. About this time, he will have to decide upon the size of the food portions, so that he can make a good choice in the size of the plates upon which he will serve the food. He should take into consideration how much surface design there will be on the plates and side dishes in order to compensate for such problems as smaller portions. Each plate of food should have a full and satisfying appearance. There will be a similar decision concerning the selection of the silverware or stainless steel, not only for quality and price, but also for designs that relate to the style of the interior set forth by the name, the sign, the menu, and so forth.

Also at this time, the owner must balance the length of his lease against the length of service to be secured from the fixtures, furniture, and equipment to be purchased. The efficacy of each of these decisions depends on its relatedness to other decisions.

COLOR SCHEME COORDINATION

While the owner is busy choosing pots, pans, and cooking equipment (which have no relationship to the interior or the front of the restaurant), he must also consider a predominate color scheme for the total interior package. Probably, he hasn't even begun to study upholstery fabrics, draperies, carpetings, tablecloths, napkins, the various wood and metal finishes of the furniture, etc. So he is really not familiar with the color ranges he will be able to use in making his selections.

The owner who does not have the experience of a professional interior designer may look at the color charts of one menu printer and feel he has gone a great distance by comparing that with the tablecloth and napkin colors. But this, of course, is only the beginning. These same colors may well be repeated in the sign, the billboard, and other types of advertising.

Generally speaking, the owner/designer should make his first selection of that material—whether it is the carpeting, the draperies, or the wallpaper—in which he desires to use a large-scale design. From that he may make a determination of how best to apply color to the other materials to be purchased.

Suppose that he purchases a large-patterned carpeting. His next step may be to order a textured or smaller-patterned wallpaper. Finally he may move on to a tweed or solid-colored drapery. Tweed or fine-textured upholstery materials may be selected for the backs, if not the seats and backs, of the couches, booths, and chairs.

From this beginning, the owner may carry the colors of carpeting throughout many other areas, including the tablecloths, napkins, menus, wood finishes, paint colors, ceiling materials, and chinaware.

CARPETING

Before looking at carpetings, the owner must decide room size and the number of people to be seated to know how far he may go in making his selections. He must now make these selections only from those lines that will pass the most rigid of flamability tests. If the rooms are large, they are classed as places of assembly, and he will have to select from carpetings that are woven of inherently flameproof fibers. Offhand, it doesn't sound too restrictive, but it actually is quite a limiting factor. The manufacturer's carpet designs are governed by the colors supplied by yarn producers. A manufacturer of yarns that are flameproof will have only a very limited number of colors to offer. The owner who does not know this may suddenly find that there are very few carpeting colors from which he may choose. He will have to review all the related color purchases, starting with the sign on the front of the building, menus, tablecloths and napkins, and wood finishes on the furniture. There is usually a long waiting period for the arrival of carpeting. Certainly, this is true for a carpeting that is woven to order as in the case of fine restaurants. So it then becomes important to have placed the carpet order early, notwithstanding the limitations it may place on the choice of colors for all other items to be secured.

Carpetings come in solid colors, tweeds, stripes, florals, damask designs, a myriad of period styles, and contemporary patterns. Because of their excellent resistance to abrasion, nylon fibers are favored over wool and acrylic fibers. They aren't as easily cleaned, however. Therefore blends of nylon and wool fibers can be counted on for good performance both in terms of resistance to wear and ease of maintenance. For finer dining rooms, many carpetings are woven to order. A blend of 60 percent wool and 40 percent nylon is recommended. Alternately, 70 percent wool and 30 percent nylon is used. From the standpoint of ease in cleaning, carpetings with low pile height and dense weave are favored. Also, carpetings in which the fibers are woven through the back, such as broadloom or Axminster, are superior to those that are merely tufted through a polypropylene sheet and cemented to burlap or another stiffener for support.

In the lower price range, solid colors and tweeds are found more readily than the large-pattern designs. This is basically because of the limitations of the weaving process. Wanting to provide larger-pattern designs on the cheaper products, manufacturers have turned to dyeing or printing designs on the simpler, tufted carpet weaves. But at this moment, the industry has not yet reached maturity in this area. Most patterns look like cheap imitations of the finer woven-through-the-back designs.

CHOOSING FURNITURE

As his own interior designer/decorator, the owner will be faced with the need for determining the traffic flow in the restaurant, the size and shape of all tables, and the proper distribution of the various-sized tables. The owner will wish to ensure flexibility in the seating of different-sized parties in every area of the floor plan. This also is about the time he will have to decide the design of his seating pieces. Are there to be side chairs or armchairs? Are there to be side chairs, armchairs, and couches? Are the couches to be long French bench arrangements or booths for two or four persons? Are these booths or couches to be horseshoe-shaped or square-shaped?

In making these decisions, the restaurateur should be aware not only of sitting comfort but also of adherence to the overall theme. He should be careful in the choice of woods as well as wood finishes and fabrics. Fabric color selection may be limited because of the need for practicality. Resistance to abrasion and spotting, for example, is an important consideration.

Many firms may manufacture chairs that photograph alike. Few of them are capable of manufacturing chairs in the particular style the owner may prefer and of a quality that will stand up under many years of hard usage.

But how is the restaurant owner to know which is the right manufacturer and which is the wrong one? How is he to know which is the safe wood and which is the one that is unsafe? For example, birch and beech provide very hard surfaces with a very close grain. They do not readily splinter. But oak, which you may select for a strong grain character and husky look, and hickory will readily splinter. The resulting jagged portions of the chair or table legs can damage hosiery and other items of clothing.

CHAIR CONSTRUCTION

Then there is the question of chair construction. A Windsor chair, which includes the captain's type and which design enjoys at this moment a bit too much popularity, is the weakest of all chair constructions. The strength of the Windsor chair resides in the joinery of the spindles —how they are secured into the wood seat and into the arm rail. In the case of poorly made Windsors (which comprise about 85 percent of all Windsor chairs that are produced), the four legs and the multiple arm spindles are glued into holes that are perhaps only ½-inch deep in a seat that may have only a thickness of 1 inch to begin with. This is hardly good joinery. It is unsafe, and the chair will fall apart within the first six months with any kind of heavy usage. In contrast, a truly well-constructed Windsor chair should last twenty to thirty years.

How is the owner to know this? How is he to know how to determine the strength of the joinery, an all important factor in determining the worth of his chair purchase? One clue is that the manufacturer who uses the thickest seat might well be doing the best joinery. At least, he has put more money into the wood in the seating than has the manufacturer of cheaper products. There is more seat thickness into which to drill and fasten the legs and arm spindles. Even then, if these spindles are not securely glued, they may come loose. In some of the very best traditional Windsor chairs, the wood spindles, if not certain key arm spindles, go completely through the seat. They are further secured, beyond the normal gluing, by a spline driven into the split end of the spindle as it spreads beyond the top of the seat. It is then chizzled off smoothly, sanded, and finished, providing a further mark of the integrity of the maker and the quality of the product.

However, watch for those manufacturers who practice either of the following methods of deceiving the buyer on this point. Certain manufacturers make up a mock or imitation splined joint. They drill the fake joint into the top of the seat where one might expect the four legs to reappear as though they had come through the wood to fool the buyer into thinking he has gone to the trouble of bringing the legs all the way through the seat and installing splines in the exposed ends.

Another method of tricking the buyer is to use a ¾- to 1-inch thick wood slab for the main bulk of the seat and then heavily roll the front edge by adding a false wood strip to make it appear thicker than it really is.

These points are all in connection with the purchase of captain's chairs which are a type of Windsor chair construction. They do not apply in the same way to chairs that are constructed with box seats or to those that are assembled of steam-bent parts. The combination owner/manager/interior decorator is seldom aware of these falsifications when selecting his seating units. He may be in greater trouble, however, when he selects the couches or booth seating units. It is here that more fakery can be found than in any other item of furniture.

BENCH AND BOOTH CONSTRUCTION

The buyer sees a picture or a catalog cut of a booth. Perhaps he even sits in an actual unit. He then feels that all is well and makes the purchase. He then need only select the covering material for quality, color, design, and practical performance. But the inside of most benches and booths is completely hollow, a fact not known by the buyer before the purchase. A booth manufacturer, a merchant who handles booths regularly, or an interior designer should know what construction to expect inside the bench or the booth. Often this fact is only discovered when the units are opened up for their first repairs.

Can you imagine how many owners of restaurants know the size tacks and kind of fastening to be used for continual good performance in the type of spring foundation that is advertised in the catalog? If you were in the know, you would disregard any maker who uses what the upholsterers call a "one-whack" tack in place of a tack that takes as many as eight hammerings in order to be secured into the wood properly. The one-whack tack allows for the furniture to be delivered, set in place, and used for a very short time before the true story is told. The springs simply start to loosen up and shortly thereafter fall out of place.

Suppose you are sufficiently lucky to know the gauge and type of wire to be used and the type of spring coil or strand to be selected. The story is not complete until you are able to select the proper insulation at the top of the spring foundation. The proper insulation over a spring seat when used for commercial purposes is an 8- to 12-ounce duck. This is securely sewn on top of each and every spring strand or coil. The tying should be done many times and with the strongest-quality tying twine.

The insulation is not complete unless a prefabricated sisal or jute pad is presewn over the duck-covered spring platform and further secured around the edges of the hardwood frame. Even the quality of the edge roll is important. Without a good edge roll, the fabric covering may be cut through by the sharp edge of the hardwood frame. A formed-paper edging is not quite as good as a jute roll enclosed in burlap pretacked above the insulating pad onto the hardwood frame. Above these basic materials there should be a final layer of a spring-providing resilient pad of 1½- to 2-inch thick sponge rubber. It should not be foam rubber, which is a cheaper substitute. It may, however, be a top quality, firm density, polyfoam. But there are many grades of rubber and many grades of polyfoam substitutes. The rubber should be live and new, not reconstituted or reprocessed.

The wood framework that is concealed within the upholstered items should be of hardwood, securely joined by multiple dowels or mortise and tenon construction. It should be further secured by heavy corner blocks and cross struts. If a leg-style base is used instead of a closed-in box base, the legs should not be screwed on the bottom of the frame. They should extend upward into the box frame to act as corner blocks and be screwed and glued within the frame itself. Those turned or otherwise fashioned decorative legs that are merely screwed into the bottom of the wood frame will loosen up and break off either after a short term of being moved about at the restaurant site or even within the period of delivery to the restaurant.

THE FINAL PICTURE

By the time the owner/designer begins to study the relationship between the wall coverings, draperies, and carpetings, he already has too many subjects in limbo. That is, he cannot make a final decision on any one item without understanding the limitations that exist in decisions on the balance of the materials. This all comes at a time when he is designing and furnishing his kitchen. He is ordering china, glassware, silverware, pots, pans, and kettles—everything from toothpicks to light fixtures. Yet he must do a good job as his own interior designer. The interior is the first thing people will see. They will judge the quality of the restaurant by the interior. If he is to match the efficiency of a professional interior designer, the restaurateur must carry with him to his wallpaper source complete sets of literature and color charts for the many other products he must buy. Also, he cannot make a final judgment on any one of these purchases without ensuring that he will be able to obtain the wallpaper, carpeting, or draperies that go with the balance of the decorative items under consideration.

When he takes over the role of interior designer, the owner should know that the person who does this work professionally will have as many as forty or fifty books of papers from which to make choices. The professional will have had some experience as to which of these lines he must look in order to find the type of paper that carries out the main theme of the restaurant. He should be advised at this time that he may have the wallpapers treated to resist food stains and perspiration oils. Only washable wallpapers should be used in a commercial installation.

The final choices on a number of items, including wallpaper

and carpeting, have to interrelate well, not only in design but in color. The moods portrayed by each of the materials need to be correlated and must carry out the main theme of the interior design.

It is not usual for a restaurant owner to be in touch with only one merchant in each of these fields. He probably will have contacted three or so sales representatives in each field. Think of what is beginning to happen to his time! He is involved with several merchants competing with each other for the award of a contract in each field. To make matters worse, each manufacturer has a different time lag on final product delivery. Quite often, the best quality manufacturer may take the longest time to deliver. The owner considers making his purchasing decisions without regard for the need of correlating elements, but rather with the main purpose of getting the goods in on time. He starts to place orders according to how long it will take to get the products. Then his purchasing program falls completely out of line with the initial intention of carefully relating the purchases to the whole picture.

At about this same time, the restaurant operator will want to look into the type and style of uniforms for waiters and waitresses. If he wants them to be custom-made, they will have to be one of the very first things to be placed on order. Again, this procedure is at odds with his program of coordinating elements and only making purchases when he can see the whole picture.

The fact is that the owner who tries to be investor, owner, operator, and interior designer seldom sees the whole picture. This is because he impractically takes each step either as a result of the urging of the most persuasive sales representative or simply because one product merchant contacted him before another. What a way to go about things!

But you must have guessed by this time that interior design is *not* really handled in the best manner when this work is done by the owner. He has his hands full making decisions on materials and supplies for the restaurant and in hiring and training personnel. He will probably be able to do no more than order those items for which he is pressured to place contracts. This is truly, then, a shortsighted way of handling a most important and sizable investment.

Chapter 3

Decor to Fit the Trade

One of the first decisions the restaurant owner must face is what type of customer he wishes to attract and how he will secure this trade through the design of the interior. The three examples of full-service dining rooms described in this chapter range in style from farmhouse to formal. They illustrate how three different types of clientele—a family trade in the country, a mixed trade in the city, and a formal dinner trade in the city—can be designed for.

A RURAL FAMILY RESTAURANT

Our first example is a restaurant located in a rural district. A visit here is preceded by a long drive into the country. Typically, this type of dining place may be situated in an old farmhouse or an interestingly designed barn which has been remodeled to provide rooms for country-style dining. In the particular case we have selected, no alcoholic beverages are sold. The basic idea is to provide family-style dining in a wholesome atmosphere for the entire family. The waiters and waitresses

Fig. 3–1 In this remodeled, farm-style building, the fireplace, hayrack wheel chandeliers, and seating treatment set the rural theme.

are in early American costume, and the total interior reminds us of the colonies and of early America. People come from larger cities for a day in the country, and the designer provides them with what they expect to see. Everything within the interior reminds the diner of a visit to the farm. Thus the designer is creating here "decor to fit the trade."

In this example, the interiors of a farm-style business building in a small town were remodeled into a wayside restaurant. The spaces were already divided into several rooms. It was the job of the designer to open up the smaller rooms on to a central corridor, transforming them into interesting, intimate dining niches and public dining rooms.

Iron wheels from an authentic hayrack have been removed and remodeled into chandeliers. These hang close to a very low ceiling in one of the public dining spaces in the center of the several rooms. (See Fig. 3–1.) Flat rocks from a woodland creek are used to face a wide-mouthed, open fireplace. The fireplace is framed in cherry wood moldings of a simple, early American style. Country flavor is increased with the hanging of a houndstooth fabric skirt under the mantle shelf. The mantle shelf displays a copper pot with heavy, green foliage, a pair of early American brass candlesticks, and two authentic pheasants. The balance of the room continues to remind the diner of farm-style early America. The designer disguises the air-conditioning chambers by encircling them with random-width cherry planks.

A typical fireside bench, called a *settle*, may be seen, in Fig. 3–1, to form a portion of the wall treatment. It creates an interesting hideaway seating unit, accommodating four small, two-person tables. With the tables pushed together, the unit is equipped to handle one or two larger parties. The mood of a Shaker or a Quaker home is intensified by the rigidity of the design of the Windsor chairs. Some chairs have homespun-fabric back coverings. In others, the wood spindles are exposed. While several chairs are without arms, there is an equal number that are armchairs. Much of the woodwork of the seats, backs, and scrolled ends of the settle is exposed. Hanging cushions provide softness and comfort.

Wallpaper, an authentic reproduction of an early American print featuring fruit basket designs, is used in part to repeat the colors of the houndstooth mantle skirt and of the chair cushion.

Fig. 3–2 illustrates how when two rooms are too small to be of value, a separating wall can be opened up to make the two rooms into one. Wood beams and vertical paneling that divide the areas into more interesting designs continue the farm theme. A checkered pattern, reminiscent of checkered tablecloths, is employed in the overdraperies. The draperies are capped by a straight, boxed-in cornice covered in the same material. In this particular interior, the window treatment disguises an unpleasant view of the wrong end of a cow barn beyond.

The wallpaper in this cherry-paneled room is deep red-brown. The chandeliers are originally painted red and then glazed over with a brown wash coat. This treatment results in what is termed an *antique,* or *distressed,* finish. Early American bannister-back Windsor chairs are used in this room only. Also featured are pictures of two pairs of hunting dogs—one of Springers and one of Irish Setters . . . an appeal to "hunters."

We see in Fig. 3–3 how the designer uses a combination of traditional wood framing and quaint wallpapers to carry out the farmhouse style. Oversize chandeliers cover a wide portion of the ceiling in this small area. At the same time that they light the various dining

Fig. 3–2 Two small rooms are effectively opened up into one room. The early American mood is emphasized with checkered draperies and pictures of hunting dogs.

Fig. 3–3 Varied lighting treatments add to the comfort of guests. Traditional wallpapers and doorway treatments provide interesting eye appeal.

tables, the chandeliers also give aesthetic enjoyment. People enjoy sitting under lanterns, lamps, or chandeliers more than sitting at a distance looking back at them. Too often, the owner may make the mistake of using a chandelier for total room lighting. And if such a fixture is too small, the lights have to be kept at a high intensity. Although they may provide proper illumination for those who sit beneath, the glare to those who must look at them from other areas may be intolerable. With many, widespread lights and some built-in lights, no one light bulb must be so brilliantly illuminated as to be objectionable.

The country style of a wayside inn of this type might be the goal, then, of a restaurant operator whose trade comes from some distance and is comprised mainly of families. The details found in this interior entertain both the youngsters and the older members of a family. The hayrack wheels are conversation pieces for the young people, while they bring back pleasant memories to the senior citizens. A rock-faced fireplace appeals to the total family. Pheasants, hunting dogs, and quaint, country-style decor combine to tell the story customers expect to experience when driving into the country for dinner. Such an interior design goes well in a restaurant that does not sell alcoholic beverages. The customers know ahead of time that if they do not drink in a family group, in this particular restaurant they will not be embarrassed with the request for cocktail orders.

A FRENCH COUNTRY HOUSE IN THE CITY

If the restaurant owner intends to attract a large trade in a major metropolitan area, he may well depend on a farmhouse style, but with some added sophistication. Let's examine the interior decor of a country-style restaurant of French origin. It is designed to appeal to the maximum number of diners for the maximum number of times they will want to dine out. In Fig. 3–4 we see how the room is situated in connection with an entering corridor. The corridor is wide and curved; it acts as a promenade for the guest, who may from there progress to any of the various dining rooms beyond. One of these rooms is illustrated in Figs. 3–4, 3–5, and 3–6.

In selecting a feature chandelier, the owner or his designer can derive a two-fold benefit from the fixture by adding supplementary fixtures to provide general illumination. If the designer fills the basic lighting needs with concealed or built-in lighting fixtures, the whole ceiling is then in shadow. This ceiling-in-shadow effect then may be interestingly, even excitingly, decorated by light patterns thrown upon the ceiling by the chandelier. Fig. 3–4 is an example of a situation where concealed down-lighting blankets the dining spaces below. A hand-wrought, black chandelier not only is a featured decoration itself, but also plays a beautiful pattern of light and shadow on the ceiling above.

Fig. 3–4 The striking ceiling treatments in this French country-style restaurant provide light, define dining areas, and create an exciting, intimate mood.

About ninety percent of all interior ceilings are white or off-white in color. Years ago, this was done in order to allow the ceiling to increase the effectiveness of whatever lighting system was used. It was necessary to reflect the light. However, we know today that that is not sufficiently important to offset advantages in the use of colors other than white. In this example, dark brown beams encircle the room. While the main ceiling is antique white, the beams set apart areas that are of a deep wood tone. This provides a sheltering effect for the diners who occupy seats around the perimeter of the room. The remaining, lighter ceiling acts as a necessary relief to the heaviness of the deeper tones.

The ceiling is a case of "a little of one with t'other." You can see this philosophy in other facets of the room, such as the wall treatments. They are, for the main part, cherry panelings. French scrolled moldings trim them off and set apart areas for wallpapers. Then pictures are hung over the wallpaper and the wood paneling as needed to complete the design.

In each of the three corners of this triangular-shaped room, access to which is from the curved-bar corridor, there are wide open shelves in corner cases. In these corner cases are displayed various items that add to the style of the room. In one case there are a glass-enclosed model of a miniature boat of antique date; some small, framed pictures; goblets; and candlesticks. In another there are fighting cocks, hammered-brass platters, fruit jars, and a row of Tom-and-Jerry cups.

The decorating philosophy is carried through with the French scrolled couches. Here and there they form booths for four. Then they continue on as French benches to provide a variety of seating accommodations. Armchairs are pulled up to the French benches and are used again in the center of the room completely separate from the booths.

Fig. 3–5 shows some of the details of the woodwork and couches and how they relate to each other. A not too expensive ¼-inch thick cherry-veneered panel of plywood is cemented directly to a plastered wall. Then, raised moldings are applied over the ¼-inch plywood to give the effect of individually tailored panels. In certain areas, wallpaper then merely fills in between the moldings. The point of contact with the ceiling is trimmed by a heavy, wood cornice.

To get the best effect in a wood-paneled room, simple staining should be avoided. With a simple, penetrating stain, the woodwork receives the coloring in a random and uneven fashion. The wood should be given a light-tinted toner-coat of water stain and then sanded with six-0 paper. Next, it should be sealed with a half-alcohol half-white shellac mix. Spray on the mix to get a uniform effect. This coat is important as it controls the degree of absorption of the final stain or glaze. Treated in this way, paneling exhibits the "hand of the craftsman" rather than the "will of the wood."

After the sanding of the sealer coat (to which some color pigment has been added) the final, glazing stain is applied. This is a pigmented, oil stain or glaze which appears somewhat like a thinned-out, muddy wash. It is allowed to dry for a couple of minutes. Then the wood finisher wipes off most of the stain. Some stain is allowed to remain in the corners and crevices of the wood moldings at the edges of the panels to highlight the centers of the panels and add an extra dimension to the finished appearance. The final coatings may be of clear, flat lacquer or of semi-gloss varnish. This may be the wood finisher's choice as they are equivalents. The lacquer is normally sprayed on and needs no final sanding, while the varnish is normally brushed on and picks up some dust or small particles on account of the brush application.

The overhead beams should be paint-stained in a finish that is

Fig. 3–5 Corner shelves feature carefully chosen items that provide a focal point for the diner. Pictures in heavily ornamented frames reinforce the French theme.

deeper, darker, rougher, and duller, exhibiting none of the fire of the wall panels. The beams will thereby have a more structural look.

For many years, a tight tailoring together of elements of interior design was popular. Now, the interplay among the important elements of interior structure is seen as a valuable asset. A prime example, shown in Fig. 3–6, is the overlapping of the straight, wood moldings at the base of the wall panelings with the crest of the curved moldings of

Fig. 3–6 The technique of overlapping designs is seen in how the curved-back couches are made to relate to the straight wood wall moldings.

the couches below. We formerly tailored these tightly together so it appeared as though the couch grew out of the wall. A straight, wood molding on the wall matched a straight, wood molding on the top of the couch.

We later found that greater value was obtained by giving a clear indication that the one item, the couch work, was definitely not a part of the wall. It deserved its own identity. It was adjusted to the shape of the room but did not become an actual portion of a wall. This overplaying of designs again is displayed by hanging a painting in a quite elaborate, feature-type picture frame on an already heavily decorated, wallpapered surface. All this exists within a rather exciting series of surrounding wood panels. The art of this technique is in knowing how far to go with design-upon-design and then knowing how to rest the eye with other views within the same room.

This farmhouse style should attract a more sophisticated trade in a larger metropolitan area. It is informal, with its brick-faced, copper-hooded fireplace and sunken, flagstone-paved pit surrounding the hearth at the entrance. But it has a grander look than the rural farmhouse, since it caters less to families and more to those who expect to purchase cocktails, wine, or ale with their food.

The restaurant operator may then compare the farmhouse type of family-style dining with the country-style French look in the city. He can carry this comparison still further with a look at a completely formal style of dining room.

A FORMAL DINING ROOM

Whether in the heart of a city, in the suburbs, or in a nearby town, the designer can well apply a formal style to a dining room. The purpose is to attract those diners who wish to dress up for a special dining experience. Formal designs of this sort may be used in landmark residences. They are, moreover, typical of private clubs, country clubs, or city clubs.

In this example of a formal dining room, we see a style of woodwork that is normally attributed to the architect or the interior designer who handles both interior architecture and the selection of the furnishings. Formality is somewhat reduced by giving an unexpected turnabout to a typical interior paint scheme. Instead of the traditional white columns and overhead beams and wainscotings, the designer has specified all woodwork to be parrot green, and to be overglazed to highlight and emphasize the panels. These are combined with beige-white walls in one room. The adjacent room or alcove is covered with a paper of green rattan diagonal designs on a beige-white background. (See Figs. 3–7 and 3–8.)

Fig. 3—7 A daring use of color on wood columns, beams, and wainscoting is combined with rattan-designed wallpaper to create interest and diversity in this formal dining room.

Fig. 3—8 The cool, green and white color scheme is complemented by the wooden chairs, the floor covering, and the fabric used on chair backs.

The overdraperies in both rooms are a floral print that repeats the basic beige, off-white, and green. The floor, chair coverings, and wood finish of the chairs form warm complements to this otherwise cool surrounding. The seats of some side chairs and the seats and backs of some armchairs are covered with a deep Brunswick red-brown nylon tweed. The carpet is woven in a matching color. The mahogany wood of the Chippendale ladderback chairs completes the warm complement to the main room scheme. Antique brass chandeliers shown in Fig. 3–8 are hung surprisingly low over the tables to bring an extra comforting effect into the center of the main dining area. The brass chandeliers are subdued in tone by the use of small wattage lights within individual cloth covered shades.

Comparing this example of the completely formal type of dining room with the two informal styles described earlier in this chapter may help the restaurant owner decide the best direction for the design of his interior. Location, type of clientele he seeks, frequency with which he hopes they will dine with him, all will have a bearing on his determination of the most effective interior style.

Chapter 4

The New Look

The design of a new restaurant or the redesign of an existing one, whether handled by the owner or by a professional restaurant designer, is certainly of equal importance to the quality of the food to be served. In the case of the fast food restaurant, the designer may follow the crowd and study those who are currently successful in this field. It is in this area, if in any, that styles change constantly. The appeal is to a younger customer who may not know which style he enjoys the most. This type of customer is "learning." So, there is a greater need for remodeling, restyling, renovating, and changing themes in the fast food area than in the full-service dining field.

On the other hand, in the full-service dining room, the businessman dines or entertains other business people, the husband and wife dine together or meet with friends. There is little need to make constant changes in or total revisions of the style of the interior. Once an interior design image is decided upon, the owner may retain it for many years, making only small changes and surface improvements as time goes on. The good design of full-service dining rooms has been well-known for many years. Once the restaurant owner has decided upon a well-tested and traditional theme, he may count on it to serve him well for twenty-five years or more.

THE NEED FOR REMODELING

However, he may also, while keeping to the same general theme, make refreshing changes in the surface decor, wall art, and fixtures. These small surface changes are always appreciated by the clientele. The majority of full-service restaurants are poorly designed, perhaps because they have not had proper overall planning from the beginning. Improvements made in most restaurants are appreciated by the regular customers. Customers not only enjoy the new decor, they also realize that it is a mark of success for "their" restaurant to be able to make the improvements. Then, too, the actual remodeling work indicates to potential new customers that things are happening. In this way, a bid is made for the continued attention and future business.

A total renovation, of course, not only brings in the old customers. Many new people succumb to the idea of investigating or exploring the new look of the restaurant interior.

A CASE IN POINT

Illustrations on these pages are taken in a family restaurant that has been doing an excellent business for fifty years or more. The present owners, who are the sons of the founder, felt a need for expanding. Certain front rooms of the multi-room restaurant had not been redecorated for about twenty-five years. They felt, therefore, that they should plan a thorough face-lifting of at least one of the rooms. Then, they planned to add on a totally new room to take care of the increased traffic expected. After remodeling one room and adding on another, they decided to procede with the remodeling of another three dining rooms. We will examine the handling of the main bar and cocktail lounge in the front of the restaurant complex. Figs. 4–1 and 4–2 show how the remodeling of the existing cocktail bar and lounge appeared when completed. Figs. 4–3 and 4–4 illustrate the interior of the new room that was added, access to which is through the remodeled cocktail lounge.

THE BAR: REDESIGNING WITHOUT RENOVATING

The bar that is illustrated here was designed and built by the author about twenty-five years before the present remodeling. In most restaurant remodeling programs, it is seldom necessary to make change for the sake of change in the bar proper. To move a bar about or change its shape is normally not necessary.

First, the owner or designer must look into the cost of making a change to the equipment beneath the bar—bottle boxes, coolers, cocktail mixing stations, sinks, drains, and other facilities that are tied into the water lines and drains in the floor. Should a designer plan to change the location or the shape of the bar, it would be well to ask him to consider instead redesigning the overall surface appearance of the bar in its present location. The cost of tearing up the floor for water, drain, and electricity will add tremendously to your remodeling bill. Then, too, stainless steel equipment such as bottle boxes and refrigerators do not go out of style or wear out as quickly as do the furniture and furnishings in the room. A skilled restaurant designer would try to respect the existing location, shape, and size of a bar. He should rather devote his attention to the ways in which he may restyle the total interior, including the bar. He should use resurfacing materials and decorations that carry the new theme into the existing positions of these critically and (hopefully) permanently located facilities.

In the case of the interior in Fig. 4–1, twenty-five years earlier we had made a design point of setting the bar at an angle in the corner of the room . . . and a jogged angle as well. It was originally planned to follow the natural traffic pattern of the customers. But customers don't walk any differently today than they did then. So, it was easy to respect the location and odd shape of the bar in this case.

However, style changes were needed. For example, years ago the back of the bar was a place to show the many and varied types of whiskies the operator had for sale. Today the emphasis is not upon how many brands of straight liquors you can offer but, more properly, how well you can mix. The restaurant operator today places emphasis on cocktail mixing . . . as an art. He is more likely to display crystal glasses for serving cocktails than to display liquor bottles. In this case, wanting to carry out a French farmhouse style, we designed French provincial cabinets for the rear wall to replace the earlier, ponderous upper back-bar. In a typical French country manner, material stretched on tight rods was used to eliminate a portion of the view of items stored in the cabinets. The cabinets are lighted. Although they are not visible in Fig. 4–1, the tops of bottles usually peep over the tops of the curtains. This gives the general impression that here is a storage place available only to a master mixer. A slight sense of mystery is evoked. In general, recipes and the craftsmanship of mixing drinks is emphasized over the ingredients and their brand names. It is good business for the restaurant owner. He sells *his* way of serving drinks instead of advertising the manufacturers' standard brand names.

Fig. 4–1 The remodeling of the original cocktail lounge and dining room does not require any changes in the bar facilities or in the location and shape of the bar proper.

To the right in Fig. 4–1, the traditional wood spindles are shown. They provide a limited view of the cocktail lounge from the lobby. Note the positioning of the angular corner bar and how it relates to the lobby. It provides, through the overhead wood and cloth canopy, a lead-in line to offer a sort of traffic direction for the guests.

All the furniture designed and built for this set of interiors twenty-five years earlier was reused. For example, the booths, in the same shape and size provided earlier, were reupholstered with smooth vinyl on the seats and a soft goods covering on the back. They were originally so sturdily constructed that they stood up well, and the cost of remodeling proved to be a better investment for the owners than buying completely new booths.

In Fig. 4–2 the reader can see how each of the remodeled booths was reused to make more effective units. The original four-seated booths were lower in height than the designer wanted for the current remodeling. So an iron framework was mounted between each of the booths. On the iron framework, a heavy, coarse monk's cloth, or friar's cloth, was installed as a curtain. On top were two highly polished brass knobs to add the finishing touch. The addition of the curtains between the four-seated booths gives additional privacy to each seating unit. More important, it did this without the bulk that would have been added by new booths with higher backs. The curtains might be described as discreet, as opposed to an obvious and compelling, partition. Then, each booth

Fig. 4–2 A touch of privacy is added to the individual four-seated booths by curtains above the backs of the booths.

features a French country-style wall light or an individually lighted painting. A surprising touch is a flamestitch type of wallpaper that is partially covered by the painting and is framed within a gentle arch. A scrolled, oak panel mounted underneath a heavy wood cornice forms the arch.

WHAT IS A COCKTAIL LOUNGE?

In typical suburban, full-service dining rooms, there is often no need to have a room set aside as a cocktail lounge. While a room may be referred to as a cocktail lounge, it is often more functional if designed to serve two purposes—cocktail lounge and dining room. So it is with this restaurant.

The deep, quilted couches and small, wood-grained plastic top tables designed for the center of the room are perfectly satisfactory for the customer who simply wishes to enjoy a cocktail. But the same tables may be set up with tablecloths and silver for dining, serving equally well for the sale of food as for the sale of drinks. For this dual-purpose room, the designer has specified all the chairs to have arms. The combination of cane-backed armchairs and deep, quilted-back couches, with tables set up for two people at each station, invites the customer to use the space for cocktails. At the same time, it is suited handsomely for the serving of food. The long, straight French bench with curved ends on either side provides that which we so highly recommend—the freedom to push together smaller tables to create seating for a party of four, six, or eight. (See Fig. 4–1.) It is this flexibility that gives the restaurant operator the option to sell each seat to its maximum contribution to the total day's volume. Here it is important to mention that it is the job of the restaurant designer to create this seating flexibility. But it is the owner's responsibility, either personally or through a carefully selected hostess or host, to efficiently use this seating flexibility to get the maximum return for the house.

In this remodeled interior, the hostess has numerous places for single individuals or parties of two to sit and be served. She provides these guests with a booth that can seat four persons only when they have rejected the seating arrangement for two and refuse to accept it. Naturally, seating arrangements have to be made smoothly, gracefully, and without offending the customer. However, every time the host or hostess slips up in this department, fifty percent of the seating capacity is wasted.

ROOM MEETS ROOM

We can describe the threshold between two rooms as that area in which one room meets another via some kind of doorway. For as many as fifty years, we have known that if you want to get the maximum trade, you do not create any more steps at the entrance to your place of business than are necessary. Surely for a supermarket and even for a small fast food restaurant, this continues to be true. The steps at the entrance to a place of business form a kind of threshold. The actual board or metal plate at the floor line, where one surface changes to another, is perhaps the best known threshold. However, certain other design elements are also represented by this name. The frame of a door is one. The door itself is another. The combination of a door and door frame is an even more distinct one. If the door and frame are heavy or if there is a strong contrast in color, design, or texture from the first area to the second, a very distinct threshold exists, from a design point of view. It is here that a potential customer faces the possibility of change. He is made to pause mentally, perhaps physically, to reconsider whether he wants to advance into a new area.

For this reason, we recommend avoiding at the threshold any design elements that cause the customer to pause, stop, and reflect and that generally challenge his desire to proceed further.

Instead, we recommend a "holdover" technique. The illustrations here show the use of this technique. As we move from the existing cocktail bar and lounge into a new combination cocktail lounge and dining room, we see that some of the important design elements are held over or carried through into the newly added room. Carrying over certain designs, colors, and other facets of one interior from one room into another adjacent area makes it easier for the guest to decide to advance into the next room. In Fig. 4–1 we see a decorative ceiling fixture in the French country style which has also been used in the new room shown in Figs. 4–3 and 4–4. Not only the design of the fixture but also ceiling height is the same.

In Fig. 4–3 we can see that there is actually no doorway between the two rooms and no door frame. Instead, there are folding screens that seem merely to be parted to offer access to the new room. This parting of the screens at the juncture of the two rooms is handled in a casual manner. There is no real evidence of a door or a doorway. This, then, invites the guest to move freely from one room to the other. The screens are designed to match those of the upper back-bar in the same room. They are further softened by a drapery hanging on the new room side of the screens (not shown in the illustration). When there is not

Fig. 4–3 French country-style folding screens seem merely to part to provide access to a newly added dining room. It is important to avoid the look of conventional doors and doorways when inviting guests into new areas. When the new dining room is not open for traffic, the curtains are pulled together behind the folding screens . . . leaving no clues that there is another room beyond.

enough business to fill the new room, the curtains are drawn closed. Again, there is no evidence of a closed door. The original room looks complete—as though nothing more is offered or needed. Then, when the curtains are parted, an invitation is provided to the guest to move on into the new room . . . without challenge.

The general styling of the woodwork of the original room is carried

Fig. 4–4 In the new room, the oval-back country-style armchairs are a carryover from the matching oval-back bar stools in the remodeled cocktail lounge.

over into the new room as part of the holdover technique. (See Fig. 4–4.) The heavy cornices of the cocktail lounge are supplemented with beams of the same timber and wood tone. The French, oval-back bar stools of the original room are developed into matching armchairs in the new room. They show up with different material on the seats and backs, and quilted back rests. The twenty-five-year-old booths used in the original room are restyled and carried over into the new room as another holdover. In addition, the iron frames with the brass knobs and the separating curtains between the booths are carried over. Changes are made only in the color of these cartridge-roll booth backs. In the new room, they are of plaid, woven soft goods. The colors of the plaid relate to the new drapery treatment for the mock windows on the long wall.

FINISHING TOUCHES

Most of the time, strong light, such as daylight, is a deterrent to the maximum sale of cocktails. People usually do not think of having cocktails until it is evening or, more simply, until it is darker. So we not only design most interiors where cocktails are served as rooms without windows, we very often design replacements for the windows in the form of charcoal-tinted mirrors. As in Fig. 4–5, these appear to be windows that look out into a dark night view. Besides this, they reflect the people and the movement of the people in the room. They thereby provide an added dimension to the excitement and interest of dining.

You don't have to have claustrophobia to be uneasy about penetrating into a restaurant complex or a room that has no visible signs of

Fig. 4–5   Charcoal-tinted mirrors replace exterior windows and create the effect of a dark night outside—a proper time for having a cocktail.

outlet or exit. A majority of people have a measure of caution about how far they will progress into such rooms. These charcoal-tinted mirrors framed as windows produce the effect of actual windows looking out upon a night sky. They therefore serve two purposes: (1) They give relief from the otherwise closed-in look. (2) Because of the "dark night" look, they allow you to feel that it is time for a cocktail. Also, the exit sign above clearly indicates that in an emergency you can turn a door knob and the charcoal-tinted mirror will open to the exterior.

The hearth and fireplace will always remind people of a place where food is prepared. Besides that, it is historically a favorite gathering place for people who look forward to being warmed, comforted, fed, or otherwise entertained. So, a person almost expects to see one wall-designed fireplace in a full-service dining room or complex. The one pictured in these pages is typically Flemish and carries the unusual but traditional draft curtain or skirt that is found on almost all authentic Flemish fireplaces. It is also a sort of signature to this designer's work.

The remodeling of the cocktail bar in this particular restaurant was handled about twenty-five years after the original installation. Nevertheless, the design for the remodeled lounge and for the addition of the new room was handled in such a way that it should not go out of style for perhaps another twenty-five years.

The owners have a ten-year remodeling program in mind. They find that by scheduling the remodeling of various areas at intervals several years apart, they continue to successfully hold the interest of their present customers as well as attract some completely new ones who come to view "The New Look."

Chapter 5

The Importance of Good Color Selection

A primary concern of both restaurant owners and designers is the proper use of color. The importance of color to the effectiveness of a decorating scheme cannot be overemphasized. Each restaurant is a unique situation with different problems and requirements. Color can go a long way toward satisfying those requirements. We know that color is used to create a specific mood. Less obvious is the ability of color to create a sense of unity and continuity in an awkwardly shaped or sprawling room or to establish attractive distinctions between several dining areas used for differing purposes.

BASIC COLORS

In total area changes involving a number of rooms, the color scheme of one room can nicely complement the colors of another. When in doubt about colors, you cannot go too far wrong in considering the better qualities of reds and browns. Yet, it would be monotonous to carry this through all parts of the interior. The introduction of cooler colors in one area or room complements and provides relief from the schemes of reds and browns.

A safe recommendation for use of color might call for two-thirds of the interior space in reds, browns, or similar warm tones; one-third in greens and blues with the help of off-white and beige; and throughout both areas, a continuous interplay of wood elements.

This design technique was well applied in a complex of many public and private dining rooms in a suburban restaurant. There are three floors with a bar on each level. The guests enter on the second level through a rock-walled staircase lobby. They can then go either right or left to penetrate farther into the interior. It is at this juncture that a color choice is offered.

ROOMS OF MANY COLORS

A wide promenade, wood-paneled and carpeted in deep, warm red tones, gently curves off the entrance lobby to the right and develops into a traditional cocktail lounge. Three steps, although low and wide, cause the guests to step up to enter the cocktail lounge and rooms designed in warm colors. The guest who chooses not to turn right can ascend the steep circular staircase of black wrought iron positioned directly ahead. The staircase follows the curve of the grey rock walls to additional upper floors without revealing anything of their color. To balance this, the designer created a series of rooms at a lower level than the lobby and in colors that are completely complementary to those on the upper level. You enter the lower-level rooms by walking around a miniature replica of the Roman Colosseum.

The stairway to the lower level separates to go, on the one hand, to the private dining rooms beyond and, on the other hand, to the Lido Room. In strong contrast to the reds and brown wood tones of the rooms to the right of the lobby, the designers used deep aqua, turquoise, golds, and off-whites in the lower-level rooms.

In the Lido Room, hand-enameled, turned wood spindles frame the seating arrangement to create a closer relationship between the structural design and that of the furniture pieces. (See Fig. 5–1.) In order to provide more speedy table service in a room located off the lobby and away from the kitchen, the designer created a pair of master service stations. They flank a white marble-top fountain that features

Fig. 5–1 In strong contrast to the shades of red and the brown wood tones of the rooms to the right of the lobby, the designers used deep aqua, turquoise, golds, and off-whites in the Lido Room.

a classic Roman water urn. The servers are tailored of vertical-grain rosewood plastics, a single use of wood in the center of this room.

HARMONIZING COLOR AND THEMATIC DETAILS

A rattan-veneered flower box separates the passage to the private dining rooms beyond from the Lido Room. Over a bed of light green ferns and deep green topiary trees, off-white lacquered rattan posts and split rattan frames break up the long walls. (See Fig. 5–2.) Venetian lanterns hang low while white Florentine scrolled banquettes form party-style seating arrangements for special groups. Carpeting and velvet wrappings over lantern chains are of deep turquoise and lighter aqua yarns.

The Colosemo (or "Little Colosseum") is shown in Figs. 5–2 and

Fig. 5–2 In the Lido Room, Venetian lanterns hang low over white Florentine scrolled banquettes, forming flexible party-style seating arrangements for special groups.

Fig. 5–3 The Colosemo displays an Italian leaf cluster in gold with white candles. It is suspended between chains covered in aqua-colored velvet that reach from floor to ceiling.

5–3. There, an Italian leaf cluster in gold with white candles is suspended between the velvet-covered chains and reaches from floor to ceiling. Deep blue-turquoise diamond-quilted couches parallel the inside walls of the Colosemo.

Thus the guest who enters the rock-walled lobby and looks into the lower level to his left sees a set of rooms furnished in cool colors. These are complementary to the warm colors of the cocktail lounge and dining room on the upper level to his right. We might say that access is as easy to one area as to the other.

THE DINER'S CHOICE

In the example we have just examined, the use of color has been skillfully employed to create distinctive dining areas, each having its own identity. The activity of the restaurant revolves around the bar and cocktail lounge with its warm, inviting color scheme and cozy atmosphere. This is to the owner's advantage since it increases the potential for bar sales. The remaining rooms provide relief and counter-point to the mood of the bar. Here is where a customer can settle down for an enjoyable dinner with family or friends—removed from the milling crowd at the bar. When business is slow, traffic can be confined to the bar. When business is brisk, the Lido Room and the Colosemo are valuable overflow rooms.

The designer's intent is to offer the guest the ability to choose the room in which he wishes to dine. This policy must always be a flexible one, however. Unless dining rooms are reasonably well filled, there may be too much of a strain on your personnel to give good service in many separated areas. Poor service would result.

Had the designer decided to carry over the bar color scheme into the other rooms, certain advantages would have been lost. Guests that went to the left would not pass by the bar, resulting in fewer liquor sales. In addition, if traffic were light, the scattering of guests over a wide area would have been very costly in terms of service. Thus we can see that, in choosing a combination of color schemes for a large complex of rooms or for a large, irregularly shaped area, it is important to consider carefully the use to which the rooms will be put and, consequently, just how distinctive each room or area should be.

Chapter 6

Choosing Materials

How does the designer select the materials of decoration? Why does he select one over the other? What may he gain by his preferences? In choosing whether to emphasize a look of cleanliness over one of good decor, what should be considered? When is ease of maintenance an important factor? What about buying materials for their durability?

In the past, when there were fewer restaurants, interior designers often relied less on the decorative art than on the look of cleanliness. Customers were often satisfied if the interior of the restaurant merely looked clean. It did not have to appeal to them aesthetically.

WHERE "CLEANLINESS" COUNTS MOST

Times have changed, however. Cleanliness will always be important. But choosing materials simply because they have an appearance of cleanliness is not enough today. The materials must help to develop a theme, a style, or an appearance that is more welcoming than those found in the interiors of competitors. Only in a fast food operation in a subway, bus station, or airport would the designer be correct in choosing materials that placed first importance on the look of cleanliness.

In these places, the use of polished porcelain tiles, stainless steel and chrome, clear glass and plastics, will do the job better than other materials; but, perhaps this is the only area where this preference should apply. Here, too, the designer may select materials known for their ease of maintenance and ability to withstand heavy traffic and constant wear and tear.

But even when you step away from the bus stations and airports and into hamburger, fish and chips, and chicken units of the fast food field, materials in the customers' area must be selected for reasons different from these. From this point on and, in fact, in all restaurants other than those first mentioned, the competition for the customer's dollar rather radically changes the rules. (Comments made here pertain only to the customers' area and do not apply to the kitchen.)

COST, APPEARANCE, AND DURABILITY

One of the first factors in choosing furnishings and materials is the effect upon the customer. If the furnishings and materials selected do not appeal to the customer, they should not be used whether or not they are easier to clean, easier to maintain and repair, or even have a longer life than most materials. The designer must know the competition. In addition, he must have tested his selections so that they do a better job than those of his competitor in pleasing the maximum number of customers.

Another determining factor, however, in the selection of materials is the price tag. Well-designed materials are usually more expensive. Furnishings and materials that are easier to maintain and have a longer life are also usually priced higher than others. This brings us, then, to a place where the designer must exercise judgment based upon his idea of the ultimate goal. If he is designing a restaurant based on a current fad or novelty appeal, he may choose cheaper materials. In general, materials that cost less and need not wear for a long period of time satisfy the investor's need. On the other hand, if the restaurant design is of a traditional or tested style, the furnishings and materials should be selected for quality. Propriety of design, ease of maintenance, and long wearing constructions should be the determining factors.

THE LOOK OF PERMANENCE

In making selections, divide materials that thinly cover or veneer the surfaces from those that have a permanent look. It is not strange that, in this type of division, the former are lower in price and the latter are higher-priced.

On the one side, a designer may elect to paint the wall surfaces, which is, of course, the least expensive way to handle them. On this side also is the papering of the walls, which may be described as thinly veneering the walls. It is not as expensive as other treatments. Painting a concrete floor or laying down with cement an inexpensive asbestos or vinyl tile is the least expensive way to cover a floor. Many small, inexpensive chandeliers, made of cheap, stamped-out parts, that imitate finer-quality fixtures are substituted for decoration and give the appearance of adequate lighting. The investor can always find a new factory that produces the captain's chair or any other currently acceptable design cheaper than other factories. There is always a new booth maker, too, who makes his inflated units appear as acceptable as the well-constructed models of a better-quality manufacturer.

The restaurant designer who uses wood, brick, rock, tile, and other natural elements for wall coverings in developing an interior that is appealing to the trade will have to come up with a relatively high price tag. Better-quality carpeting, light fixtures, and furniture, selected for their contribution to the design theme, for their quality construction, and for the reputation of the manufacturer, will surely increase the cost of the investment. But these better-quality materials have a look of permanence as well as of quality. If selected for their contribution to the main design theme, they will add to a higher degree of acceptance by the public.

The painted interior can only go so far. The wall decoration that combines paint with wallpaper or wall vinyl also has its limitations. The sought-for customers can sense this "skin deep" manner of decorating and are not won over by it.

The ability to choose to use exposed-wood structures, moldings, and panels, together with natural stone, brick, or tile materials, and to include wall fabrics and quality papers is favored by most designers. The privilege of selecting from the product lines of the best-quality light fixture manufacturers and from the catalogs of chair, table, and booth makers that are recognized for their time-tested designs and quality construction must be the wish of every designer who hopes to secure the best results in his work. Our office prefers to interrelate interior architecture with interior design and the selection of the furnishings. Only in this way do we feel we obtain the best results.

EXAMPLE: THE USE OF WOOD

Let's examine, as an example, the effective use of one popular design material—wood. Whether it is to be employed in a one-room restaurant or a restaurant of many rooms, wood is a major contributor to the successful design of the interior. Yet wood is a relatively expensive material, many claim. In the following illustrations, we can see how the expense of wood is more than compensated for by its versatility

Fig. 6–1 Deep chestnut-stained oak panels give the room a framed-in look while apportioning off wall spaces for printed cloth panels in a country-style dining room.

and aesthetic appeal. Moreover, there are ways to achieve the look of wood without incurring all of the expense.

Wood is a natural material with which people are very well acquainted. People feel comfortable surrounded by wood. We use it to expose the structure or pseudostructural elements of a room design. Again, we use wood as a way to frame doors, windows, and mantle pieces. Wood is also used in moldings and pilasters that divide walls covered in one material from walls covered in other materials.

In Fig. 6–1 deep chestnut-stained oak panels give the room a framed-in look, while apportioning off wall spaces covered in printed cloth, in a country-style dining room. This is a reasonably costly room treatment, but it should have a lasting appeal to the customers. The room contains four corner cases that display pewter and china antiques and reproductions that colorfully repeat the theme expressed in the wall fabric and pictures. Painted chandeliers in a barn-red, distressed finish pick up yarn colors from the carpeting and the farmyard print

Fig. 6–2 Person-height wood paneling allows the designer to introduce a bold, printed fabric on the upper wall. The masculine appeal carries over into another room, where another large print is used in floor-to-ceiling draperies.

featured on one of the wall panels. The use of cafe curtains offers the guest the opportunity to watch passers-by while promising a measure of privacy to the viewer himself.

Fig. 6–2 illustrates how to add to the masculine appeal of a room. A people-height paneling literally surrounds the diner (or cocktail guest, in this case). At the same time, it holds together a series of rooms by accenting a compelling wall fabric. Fabric is used in one room above the paneling and in another room as a floor-to-ceiling wall covering.

Fig. 6–3 This round dining room has as its center a fieldstone and wood fireplace. Heavy, structural steel beams overhead are disguised by veneering with ¼-inch paneling. Thin wood panels are applied over a construction of two-by-fours on the walls of the room.

Modern methods and materials may be used to keep the cost of the wood look to a minimum. The dining room shown in Fig. 6–3 is a round one that is purposely interrupted on one side for variety and to introduce a new dining area beyond. The portion of the round dining room seen here surrounds a fieldstone and wood fireplace. The fireplace is located in the center of the point of interception of the otherwise round room. Heavy structural steel beams overhead are disguised by a veneer of ¼-inch wood paneling. The same thin wood panels are applied over

Fig. 6–4 The thrift of employing plastic beams and simplified, modern building techniques enables the designer to transform a square room into a round one at lower than expected cost.

a framework of two-by-fours on the walls that surround the room. The most expensive ingredient in this design is the carving of the wood moldings. The rich, permanent, here-to-stay look of the framed view into the interior is created nonetheless by the less expensive construction detail.

Figure 6–4 shows how this otherwise square room was inexpensively recreated into a circular form. A framework is fashioned of two-by-fours that are positioned to form the circle. The ¼″ good-one-side 4′ by 8′ long panels are fastened directly onto proper ground with nails and glue to make a curved surface. The false windows within the curved paneling are similarly constructed, using ⅛-inch thick masonite panels that are readily formed into circular shapes to give the effect of a limited exterior view.

Shaped moldings are next applied over the ¼-inch wood panels•to complete the design of the wall paneling. The application of wood moldings to divide the surfaces of the ¼-inch wood panels is aided in a large measure by staining and finishing. The panels so created are highlighted in the staining and finishing operations. This gives greater depth than would be expected from a simple nailing of wood moldings over ¼-inch paneling. A description of how to stain panels and molding appears in Chapter 3.

One of the features of this semicircular dining room is a lowered ceiling that supports a system of pseudowood beams surrounding a center core and an extensive chandelier. The beams themselves, however, and their carved finials are of prefinished plastic. These two techniques—(1) cementing ¼″ paneling over proper ground and applying moldings on the top surfaces in place of constructing the paneling in the more traditional way and (2) substituting prefinished artificial wood beams and finials for real wood fixtures on the ceilings —serve to give the ambience of wood to the circular dining room . . . at a price that is affordable.

Fig. 6–5 illustrates again a heavy reliance on wood to develop a handsome interior. Here, in a state park lodge designed by architects Pansiera, Dohme & Tillsley and Paul Clayton, A.S.I.D., exposing the

Fig. 6–5 A combination of wood construction timbers and rock walls surrounds the extended-view windows in the coffee shop of a state lodge.

very structure of the building adds a great deal to a dramatically attractive interior. Rock walls and supporting timbers that are part of the structure form an impressive setting for the restaurant interiors at the Salt Fork Lodge in Cambridge, Ohio.

There is no thin veneering of surfaces here. Every design element is part of the construction of the building proper. Also, everything is custom-made, from the handpainted mural and one-of-a-kind light fixtures to the server shelter and the design of the chairs and weaving of the carpet. Although expensive to create, it is another example of how wood and rock surfaces contribute to the overall beauty of the interior.

IS IT SUITABLE?

Regardless of the limits of your investment budget or the demands of your particular restaurant style, the designer should be able to find materials that are aesthetically pleasing as well as suitable for your specific use. The designer must have more than a firm grasp on the products available and a knowledge of their functionality. He must be able to imaginatively utilize materials in a successful and effective interior design calculated to attract the trade you desire to reach.

Chapter 7

The Private Dining Room

There are several advantages in having private dining rooms in connection with the main public dining rooms in a restaurant. Each of these advantages works in a different way to bring about a greater sales volume and profit for the owner. One is in advertising. The operator who can offer both public dining and private may appeal to dining parties of one person upwards to parties the size of the total seating capacity. You can see in the Yellow Pages of the phone book how many dining rooms advertise private parties from ten to several hundred. In other words, the owner can announce this additional service facility without increasing the advertising budget.

Another value is simply that he may cater to parties or groups of people as well as to individuals. This, in itself, has advantages from the standpoint of preselling his seating capacity. That is, the attendance of a certain number of guests is guaranteed ahead of time. He can then make savings in purchasing supplies, knowing ahead of time just what each guest will be served. This cuts down on food waste.

Then, let's look at it from a public relations angle. People who belong to clubs, societies, and fraternities, or just people who come together on special occasions as a group, may never have thought of dining in the public areas of a restaurant that offers private dining rooms. However, when invited as part of a group, these potential future guests have the opportunity to observe the interiors of the public area and to judge the quality of the foods. They may be in no other way successfully attracted to visit the restaurant except by the invitation extended through the club or organization.

Another value in having private dining room facilities is the flexibility it offers to the operator. This is of greater importance if the positioning of these rooms has been skillfully handled in the original design stage. On certain occasions, no one will have reserved the private dining rooms; on those occasions, this additional seating capacity is often needed to take care of the overflow of customers from the main public dining rooms. The private dining facilities, therefore, are useful in two ways—(1) for private parties and (2) as an overflow seating area for the main dining rooms.

POSITIONING THE PRIVATE DINING ROOM IN THE RESTAURANT LAYOUT

This brings us to the initial floor planning of the total restaurant, one that combines public dining areas and private dining rooms. It is not difficult to understand a designer's explanation of a safe, traditional layout of the interiors of a multiroom restaurant. For example, let's construct the layout for a restaurant that has two public rooms and, say, three private dining rooms, plus a cocktail lounge.

Hopefully, there is space for a reasonably large lobby or lounge which also houses the cashier and the cloakrooms and washroom facilities. (It is important that washroom facilities be handy to the incoming guest. They might not obviously face immediately upon the lounge or upon a dining room, but rather be located in a side aisle that leads off from the main lobby and dining room.)

A good location for a cocktail lounge or bar is to the left or right of the lobby. In this case, let's place the cocktail lounge to the left of the lobby. Double doors or wider openings using portieres (curtains) or some similar device quietly invite the guest to take liquid refreshment before proceeding to his table for dining. An ideal design allows **the** cocktail lounge to overflow into the main dining room. Therefore, let's place the cocktail lounge immediately adjacent to the main dining room. The bar conversations are always a little bit more exciting and interesting than dinner table talk. If there is entertainment besides, it should be able to be viewed and heard not only by those in the cocktail lounge but also by those in the main dining rooms.

Since the cocktail lounge is to the left, a corridor leading off the lobby to the right directs guests to the private dining rooms. The corridor that leads from the lobby to the private dining rooms may also be the one that houses the entrances to the washrooms. Then, as it turns a corner, it extends in a parallel manner flanking one side of the public dining rooms. This would also have a common wall with the three private dining rooms.

It is from this corridor that the guest elects to enter through one of the two open doors that lead into the public dining area. Guests using the private dining rooms also enter from this corridor.

WALLS THAT WORK FOR YOU

As we describe these corridors that distribute the guests into the private dining rooms or back into the public areas, it is well to think in terms of the wall structures themselves. Almost all private dining rooms and, in fact, the majority of all public dining rooms seem to be enclosed with solid walls. You cannot view what goes on outside the room when you are sitting in the room nor what goes on inside the room when you walk through the corridor. Try to remember a time when you have gone to a private party and have been able to view the traffic going by in the corridor outside the private dining room space. Also, think in terms of the many times when you sit within the four tightly enclosed walls of a public dining room without being able to view something on the outside of the room itself.

Restaurant designers are missing a great opportunity when they use too many solid structural-type walls through which it is impossible to see from one area to another. In our office, we consider a see-through type of wall structure of prime importance to the private dining room concept. It may be a wall of single-pane glass or double-pane, according to how much sound control is desired. It is our contention that a good portion, if not a large majority, of people who attend parties or even meetings in private dining rooms prefer to be able to view outside the room proper through at least one of the walls. This may very well be the entering wall. Through this wall of glass, then, they may see people moving about in the corridor. A set of heavy, coarse net draperies on traverse rods may be pulled across to diminish the view, so that the passersby in the corridor appear only as vague figures. And for those times when no visibility into the corridor whatsoever is wanted, there may be opaque overdraperies which completely erase the view. In other words, we believe in flexibility. The restaurant operator must have a tool that works for all occasions.

Let's look at this same design theory from the standpoint of those who walk by the corridor. From the point of view of advertising, there is a total loss when the guest in the corridor walks by a solid wall with a closed door. As far as he is concerned, the door may lead to a cupboard, an office, or a washroom; it has no special interest or significance to him. There may be a hundred people having a happy party within the closed walls. But if the guest who is walking through the corridor cannot see them, the party does not add to his enjoyment, entertainment, or enlightenment about these special private party facilities. On the other hand, when a guest walks through the corridor and can see, although vaguely through glass and coarse net curtains, this same large party of people enjoying themselves, he must be impressed with the obvious success of the restaurant and the public acceptance of its facilities. Another value of the combination glass and curtain walls that separate the public from the private rooms is that when the private dining rooms have not been reserved, they may well provide overflow seating for the main dining rooms. For these reasons, then, our office recommends the use of glass and curtains from floor to ceiling and from wall to wall on both walls of the inside corridors—facing both private rooms and public dining spaces.

THE IMPORTANCE OF A BAR

In the case of the restaurant we are creating, part of these see-through glass and curtain walls is taken up by a permanent bar that serves the first two of the three private party rooms. If you want to serve to a lively party in one or two of the three rooms—and at times open the doors to throw the three rooms into one—you will need a bar that is sizable and is also permanently set up and ready to operate. Nothing so quickly slows down the pace of a private party as a portable bar that is too small to adequately serve the crowd. Small portable bars always seem to run out of one supply or another while the guests wait impatiently and unhappily.

The liquid refreshment facility or service bar should be built between entrances to two of the private party rooms and tightly connected with a folding curtain wall or folding panel wall. In this way, when two parties are going on at the same time, the bar can serve through one side into the first room and through the other side into the second room. This may be done by splitting the bar right down the middle with the folding divider wall. Otherwise, the bar can be located at one end of a service bar room, providing two sides of the bar to serve into one room and one side to serve into the other. The manner of service may be decided upon in connection with the size of each of the two parties going on. There is no need for another bar for the third room. If you have three parties going on at the same time, the smallest can substitute a portable service bar. If there are two parties going on and one is sizable enough to occupy two rooms, the single bar can serve one room on one side and the other two rooms on the other side.

Your guests come in through the curtained, glass-faced entrance walls on either side of the service bar. The bar can be a room built from floor to ceiling with a narrow counter top and passage space through which the drinks are served. It should not intrude upon the room and should be designed just like all the other walls. That is, it should be a built-in facility, not an intrusive add-on.

Your kitchen is best located immediately behind the main public dining rooms. It should have entrances into the public rooms as well as into the corridor that leads to the private dining rooms.

There are many designs of room positioning and arrangements that are equally good. The example we developed here simply highlights some of the important points to consider in planning private dining rooms.

SAMPLE TREATMENT

Private dining rooms should be designed and stylized so that they can be used as public dining rooms in overflow situations. They should

Fig. 7–1 In a private dining room divided into the smallest spaces, each area still appears to be a complete room.

not look like "great halls" made to accommodate many people without any personal relationship to the smaller groups.

Two examples of private dining rooms are shown here. Figs. 7–1 and 7–2 illustrate the design of three private dining areas that may be opened up into one room for over 500 persons. Figs. 7–3 and 7–4 illustrate a larger private dining room that has a 1,000-person seating capacity and can be divided into three separate rooms.

The two private dining areas—those in Figs. 7–1 and 7–2 and those in Figs. 7–3 and 7–4—are located in a large complex of dining rooms; one area is immediately across the hall from the other. In this way, with all the tables and chairs removed, the space that serves food to over 500 can hold 1,000 people as a standup cocktail room—a preliminary to dining in the larger rooms across the hall.

In Fig. 7–1 we see that an extensive service bar has been built into one side wall with passageways on either side. This is sufficiently large to allow five or six bartenders to handle a large crowd. But, since it is a bar that is completely built in, it is not offensive during parties where drinks are not served.

Fig. 7–2 Partitioning mechanisms can be disguised by extending side walls out along the curtain tracks. In this way, smaller rooms seem to develop more plausibly, and the actual curtains or panels are concealed within the extended walls.

Part of the art of designing a private dining room with one wall that opens up to another private dining room is to so handle the problem that when the room is divided off into its smallest space, it will still appear to be a complete room design. You will see in Fig. 7–1 how the two huge chandeliers, with individual vaulting above and secondary ceilings surrounding the chandeliers; the black glass mirrored window designs; and the decorative wall panels make this a complete room in itself. It does not seem in any way to be just part of a larger space. This, we feel, is important.

It is valuable to use more than one feature chandelier in a small room. In this case, one of the fixtures focuses attention in a very decorative way over the speaker's end of the table; the other acts as a cocktail chandelier, hanging low among the entering guests.

An important design space that is so neglected by many interior designers is the ceiling. Special attention has been given to the design of each of the three ceilings within the three rooms in Figs. 7–1 and 7–2. When the three rooms are thrown together, they do a greater job of breaking up the huge hall into people-sized areas. People relate better to shapes and sizes that are not too large. You might think that these ceilings were too expensive to be considered by many restaurant owners. They are merely acoustic panels that are dropped to two heights. Then, acoustic panels interconnect the upper plane and the lower plane. Two slanted panels create the framework on which papier maché is mounted in place. The end result is the creation of cornices that resemble those expensively constructed from plaster or carved wood moldings.

Note also that a portion of the side walls extends out for perhaps 25 to 30 inches along the tracks of the sliding panel or curtain walls as an aid to completing each individual room design. This also decreases the amount of curtain that appears on one side of each of the three rooms so divided. (See Fig. 7–2.)

THE VERY LARGE PRIVATE DINING ROOM

Figs. 7–3 and 7–4 illustrate how to develop an interior that, although very large, relates well to people. Here the designer creates raised floor sections at each end of the long dining room to provide a better view towards the center (see Fig. 7–3). When only one-third of the room is sold as a private dining room, the elevated floor gives a preferred, loge-type seating to the guests who sit on the upper level. They can thereby view the speaker's table positioned in the center of the curtain dividing off the three rooms. Food comes in from the end walls. The guests enter each of the three rooms by going left, right, or straight forward from the large vestibule shown at the left in Fig. 7–4. At the right in Fig. 7–4 is a center stage and dance platform.

When a room is so designed, it may be sold in thirds or all together as one. Those reserving the center third have the elevated speaker's table which also acts as a dance floor and stage. Those reserving the end rooms have a long curtained wall as the centerpiece for their speaker's table. This would also be the proper place for a portable dance floor, centered upon the curtain.

In most cases, as in this one, we are confronted with low ceilings. We try to give some relief from the low ceiling by creating shallow vaults in portions of the ceiling. These vaulted areas are about 22 feet in diameter; they surround five large, Empire-style crystal and bronze chandeliers, 8½ feet in diameter. The bronze metal of the chandelier is repeated in actual bronze veneer that covers all surfaces of the vaulted area above the chandelier design proper. In this way, the fixture itself takes on an added dimension. The whole vaulted area becomes, in effect, an architectural chandelier treatment. It serves many more people than would otherwise be the case without the added vaulting means.

Fig. 7–3 Elevating part of the floor in semicircular design at the end of a long series of related private dining rooms has two advantages. When each end third is divided off as a smaller dining room, the speaker's table is centered in front of the curtained dividing wall. In this case, the semicircular loge-type seating offers as good a view as those seats closer to the speaker.

Fig. 7–4   In this private dining room, one may seat a maximum number of persons, but the room also may be divisible into three private rooms, the guests enter through a classic mirrored entrance lobby on the left. Two pairs of doors open into the end thirds of the room and one pair of doors enters into the center portion. When the room is divided, the food comes through other pairs of doors at the extreme ends of the room. The elevated stage, used for shows when the rooms are all opened up together, forms a speaker's table and dance floor for the center room or for two rooms opened together.

Although our examples in this case are of rather sizable private dining rooms, the points made within the chapter are as applicable to small as to large rooms. The restaurant owner who wisely plans to include private dining rooms in his original concept has an advantage over those who do not offer these facilities.

Chapter 8

Redesigning Interiors:
Obstacles to Overcome

When, in place of building a totally new structure, the restaurant investor works with an existing property, there are both advantages and obstacles. If the restaurateur is remodeling his own property, he may find that many of the things he had done originally may be successfully reused. In this instance, careful study of the existing interiors should be made to ensure that all things of worth are respected. The contemplated changes should replace only those features of the original design that do not fit the needs of the new interior.

There may be an advantage in securing a property that was at one time an elegant or interestingly designed residence. The handsome architecture that one finds in a fine residence would be too expensive to recreate at today's prices. The public is attracted by the idea of dining in a home environment that would have been the envy of all when it was a private residence.

When remodeling commercial properties, however, the investor is more often faced with an absence of architectural elements of value. More often than not the ceilings are too low or too high; the shape of the spaces, too long and narrow. If there are windows, they are too high and too narrow. And whatever decorative architectural elements are within the spaces do not apply to the theme that the owner plans to promote. Examples in this chapter indicate it is possible to overcome some of these obstacles.

THE LOW CEILING

Fig. 8–1 shows the interior of a restaurant redesigned from what was originally a department store. We can see how the obstacle of a too-low ceiling was overcome by the designer. On the ground floor of the store, the ceilings were extremely high. This obstacle was somewhat overcome by (1) carrying the line of the balcony over a greater portion of the lower floor in order to break the extreme height and (2) hanging large chandeliers low over the furniture and fixture groupings below.

Fig. 8–1, however, exhibits the balcony scene, where the ceilings

Fig. 8–1 Extremely low ceilings appear higher when framed with a still lower frame and edge-lit. The ceiling also benefits from light grey-blue or other cool coloring, especially as a relief from warm colors used elsewhere in the room.

were extremely low. Here the designer counted on optical illusion. Elements of a newer and a lower ceiling were built below the line of the existing one. Since the balcony dining spaces were to be used both as overflow rooms for the main dining areas and also to provide private dining spaces, the new lower ceiling carried the tracks for the movable partitions that divided these spaces.

The new lower ceiling created a wide but shallow coffer in which lighting was installed. Then, special downlighting units were built into the lower ceilings. These placed emphasis on the table and chair arrangements and on the furniture and carpeting in general, while the coffered ceiling stood out in relief above. The designer used a pale grey-blue as a "sky color" for the coffers; the rest of the interior colors were beige, off-white, cinnamon brown, and bittersweet. These colors were then carried into the cherry wood tones of the furniture and into the weaving of the carpet.

Painted tole wall lights surrounded the columns and the wall pilasters and were installed at eye level. This, together with the other design techniques, attract the attention of the guests away from the otherwise low ceilings.

DEALING WITH EXTRANEOUS STRUCTURES

Fig. 8–2 is the result of the redesigning of a four-apartment building to make it suitable for restaurant use. At the right and left, the reader may still recognize the windows that look out upon the street from spaces that were originally two apartments on the ground floor. In order for the tenants to get to the two apartments on the second floor, there had to be a central hall and staircase. The walls surrounding this hallway and staircase are necessarily of a structural nature. Besides that, the landlord in this instance wanted to continue to rent the upper floors for residential use. In the center of the picture you can see how this particular center stairway was disguised as a large, shuttered box. These shutters were softly lighted from behind. This provided a portion of the decorative lighting for the interiors.

A remnant of the main divider wall between the two first floor apartments can be seen in the form of a new rounded column. This was planted with vines and mulberry branches to carry out the theme. "Here We Go 'Round the Mulberry Bush" is printed in storybook-style

Fig. 8–2 The designer removed a wall between two ground-floor apartments and restyled the room. Woven webbing suspended from the ceiling, rattan furniture, and a "Here We Go 'Round the Mulberry Bush" centerpiece contribute to the garden theme.

lettering and colors on a parasol that contains the mulberry bush branches in an acceptable manner.

Since this was originally a residential structure, it also had the shortcoming of extremely low ceilings. In addition, the room spaces were too small and narrow. The designer pursued a solution that would handle both problems.

Room proportion is important. When a room is too narrow and too high, simply lowering the ceiling makes the room appear wider. And when the room dimensions themselves are also small, the removal of a wall to open up several rooms together will bring about a more dramatic change.

In the case of the interiors of The Mulberry Bush, grey-chartreuse plastic webbings were interwoven in a diagonal pattern about 9 inches below the existing ceilings. Then, the 9 inches of the perimeter walls above the line of the webbing and the acoustically treated ceiling itself were treated in a deep mulberry color of reduced intensity. Next, lighting cylinders that hung from the mulberry ceiling down to the height of the webbing were also painted to match the ceiling.

In this way, all lighting was deflected from the existing ceiling, as the light cylinders played upon the furniture arrangements below. This lighting was supplemented by the illuminated shutters, the wall bracket lights, and candles on the tables. Murals (not pictured here) carried out the theme of dancing around the mulberry bush. The woven webbing of the ceiling, the parasol top to the mulberry bush, and the rattan furniture more completely filled out a garden theme.

DISGUISING OUTSIZED WINDOWS

Fig. 8–3 and 8–4 show interiors that were the result of two remodeling programs. These began with an open and extensive porch area and reclaimed it as a part of the interior space. In the first remodeling

Fig. 8–3 This restaurant mocks a French country residence. The designer used panelling to make the windows appear more recessed. The cafe curtains and blinds add to the ambience with their country scenes. Brass rods support the cafe curtains, which conceal the original window sill.

(not shown here), the owners had simply plastered over the large columns and applied an enclosing wall of about 4-inch thickness between the columns to bring the former porch spaces into the interior. They installed windows at a window sill height of approximately 42 inches from the floor. The windows reached all the way to the ceiling. The owner used wallpaper and paint to complete the job.

For the second remodeling, the designer, then, had to deal with the obstacle of windows that were too high from the floor and rose to a height too near the ceiling. The designer chose a French farmhouse theme. In order to carry out the look of a farm building, he made changes in the window walls. The walls of a European farmer's house are thick and the windows, therefore, deep set. By filling in the spaces between the columns with a proper base material and applying ¼ " oak paneling scrolled in a French provincial manner, the designer overcame this part of the problem. The windows that were too high from the floor were disguised. A new low window sill height of approximately 18 inches was established; cafe curtains were hung in front of the original window sills, which were too high, to conceal them.

The material of the cafe curtains is an authentic French *toile de Jouy*, a traditional eighteenth century pattern that depicts French country scenes. This material is also used to fabricate Austrian shades that pull down from above to control the amount of sun admitted. French provincial cocktail tables and low, soft-seated lounges give the guests in the cocktail lounge end of the reclaimed porch the feeling of being entertained in a private residence. Portions of the narrow porch were also divided off by portieres (curtains) to provide private dining rooms, as shown in Fig. 8–4.

The center of the porch, which became the cocktail lounge, had another problem—the presence of an exterior rock wall of a fireplace that opened into a room to the left of the picture. By cutting a new opening into the rock wall, the designer made the fireplace into one that served both rooms. Then the rocks, which had been painted white for a period of many years, were repainted in greys and overglazed with deeper greys to restore them into their original rock coloration. To complete the picture, a U-shaped Mediterranean-style warming bench was fashioned to encircle the newly opened fireplace. It provided a

Fig. 8–4 Portions of the long and narrow newly enclosed porch area are used for private dining rooms. The central portion with its fireplace is used as both a cocktail lounge and as a gathering spot.

gathering place for those cocktailers who preferred the warmth of the fire to the cocktail lounge circle.

THE PROBLEMS OF COMMERCIAL BUILDINGS

In renting or leasing a space for restaurant use in a modern office building, there are two major obstacles to overcome. There are usually no built-in architectural elements of value that will contribute to the design of the restaurant interior, and the building codes limit the type and use of materials from which to stylize the restaurant.

Fig. 8–1 is an example. Straight, plain ceilings, walls, and floors describe the rented space. Ever tightening building codes place restrictions on all materials that are used within. Wood-paneled walls were normally built up over wood grounds that were first fastened to the walls. This left hollow spaces behind the wood paneling which have proven to be hazardous since they encourage the spread of flames.

In one sense, this has worked to the advantage of the modern investor. Wood paneling is allowed as long as it is cemented tightly to an existing wall of fireproof material. You cannot glue or cement a thick plywood panel to a wall without having it pull loose, as the walls and the wood panelings expand and contract at different rates. However, you can use very thin wood panels, the movement of which on the wall corresponds more closely to that of the movement of the wall itself.

The owner can also buy actual wood veneer laminated to canvas. This may be hung like wallpaper and still look like the richest of wood paneling treatments. In this case, which is more typical of the new and acceptable manner, ¼-inch thick three-to-five-ply paneling is cemented in large sheets directly onto the wall. Then, wood moldings are finish-nailed and glued directly on top of the wood paneling to give

Fig. 8–5 In this five-star restaurant, a plain, flat wall surface is giving a look of elegance. Quarter-inch-thick wood paneling and related moldings are glued directly to the wall. The materials and the method of application are both less expensive than traditional wood paneling.

Fig. 8–6 In the basement of a high-rise office building, a rustic tavern interior was changed into a gourmet restaurant.

the effect of divisions. The look of a wood pilaster or wood column is handled in the same manner. It can be of a different grain of wood and stained somewhat deeper so that it stands out in relief, as in Fig. 8–5. This kind of treatment happily reduces the investment of the restaurateur in the property of the owner of the building. It is definitely less expensive than installing the traditional, old-fashioned type of paneling over furring strips. Portions of the wood paneling are either omitted or, as in this case, covered over with a wallpaper or wall fabric to form a background for a collection of original oil paintings.

In the couches, which are built in sections, and in the furniture and carpetings, and of course in the paintings, the owner may invest more heavily; these do not become part of the building and may be removed at any time to a new address.

Fig. 8–6 illustrates the interior of a restaurant in the basement of another high-rise office building. In an original handling of this space, the architectural elements were determined in view of the owner's use of the space as a rustic tavern. The columns and walls were of oak wood. Oak tavern chairs and stalls added to the look of a tavern or pub. In a later program of remodeling, the restaurateur planned for a more sophisticated clientele. Changes were undertaken which would somewhat erase the look of a tavern and replace it with a look of opulence and high living.

Dull, flat, flame-red paint applied over all the wood surfaces of the original heavily beamed ceilings added richness and warmth to liven up a down-in-the-basement look. Gold stencils on white linen walls were used in a measure; a series of tongue-in-cheek line drawings were interspersed between the gold stencilings. These were both matted and framed in the same white linen as the walls. Then the massive columns, which were first framed in oak, were veneered with antique gold-veined black mirrors. Mounted on the side panels of the mirrored columns were traditional wall sconces which reflected the tiny candle lights into the black and gold mirrors.

Flame-red, frieze-covered, French scrolled love seats were installed around the perimeter of the room. Green topiary trees in brass and teakwood tubs further apportioned off each curved section of the couches. Carpeting was a marbled design of reds and beiges. Ornamental plaster chandeliers and painted shades were of the same flame color as the ceilings. The balance of the furniture, including the custom-designed gourmand stand, were covered with white leather. Table candles formed the basic lighting for the room. Accent lights on the food displays and on the accessories over the hearth supported the candle light.

In this way the designers of the Maisonette, another five-star restaurant, continued in overcoming the obstacles presented by the challenge of changing a basement first into a tavern and finally into a gourmet restaurant.

Chapter 9

Competing with the Chains

So far we have been discussing the design of sit-down, tablecloth, or full-service type restaurants. Any study of restaurant design would be incomplete if it did not acknowledge the growth of the large restaurant chains, more particularly the largest growing segment of these—the fast food restaurant.

Once a pilot model for a chain has been designed and one or two constructed, the management merely repeats the original package as often as each new installation proves successful. As in the case of McDonald's and Kentucky Fried Chicken and others, sometimes over 5,000 of these look-alikes are constructed.

Perhaps in the beginning, as many as six designs were submitted by one or more sets of designers. Thereafter, thousands of installations followed the same pattern. Everyone has, in his hometown, anywhere from one to twenty or more actual operating copies of the original pilot models. If he wishes to study the design of these restaurants, it can all be done within one day by driving about and viewing the actual installations in full operation.

THE WEAKNESSES OF THE CHAIN DESIGN

The most successful operators of fast food chain restaurants should be respected for their obvious contributions to practical restaurant operation. But, we should study them not only to observe the good, but also to discover their mistakes. Since the larger chains have so many outlets over such a broad area of the country, they have, in effect, opened wide a huge textbook to be studied by you, a potential competitor. Then, after a careful examination of this open textbook, a restaurant operator may evolve his own ideas on how to improve on the work done by the big leagues. After looking critically at McDonald's and other quick-service restaurants that specialize in hamburgers, you should not find it difficult to understand our viewpoint that each of these restaurant chains has a large Achilles' heel. There is a definite weakness in the architectural and interior designs of these chain operators.

First, let's study the movements of a potential diner during a twenty-four-hour period. When he is going to and from work, church, school, or a recreation spot or when he is simply driving directly to a restaurant to dine, he passes the chain restaurant at various times during every twenty-four-hour period. In other words, the building, as it is designed and built for the chain operator, is viewed by any and all passersby who are potential customers at all hours—not necessarily during customary dining hours. Accordingly, these restaurants are viewed by their potential customers not only during their busiest moments when they look most successful but also during their least busy moments when they look not so successful. The building itself and all that meets the eye within the property, including the interiors, create an image that impresses the potential diner in whatever way it is viewed by him most often.

Let's take one typical McDonald's restaurant where fifty to a hundred seats can be seen through glass on three sides. The dining room is located in front of the carry-out section, and the kitchen is enclosed at the back of the building. Each time the passerby looks at the McDonald's, then, he sees whatever is a true situation at the time he views the restaurant. If there is no one in the dining room at that time, it is simply an empty dining room; it appears to be a not successful dining room. If he is able to see the carry-out section behind the dining room where the clerks are waiting for customers, this must surely translate as an unsuccessful dining room plus an unsuccessful, or at least not very busy, carry-out counter.

In the case where the kitchen is enclosed behind the carry-out section, the several clerks might very well be working or talking in the kitchen if there is no business at the counter, and the passerby sees what appears to be an unsuccessful dining room, an unsuccessful carry-out section, and no signs of life. The potential customer, at least for the moment, feels sorry for the unsuccessful restaurant. He wonders whether it is because the food may not be that good or perhaps that it may be an unpopular place to go, either of which conclusions works to the disadvantage of the restaurant operator.

Now let's consider the operation of an employee in a dining room so designed. He feels more comfortable behind the scenes of a closed kitchen when there is no immediate traffic in the restaurant. Divorced from the view of the passing traffic, he feels more protected and happier in the closed-off areas. However, this. is pretty bad for management. About all management can do, other than rebuild the restaurant, is train the employees to be in positions where they can be seen by their potential customers. Then, of course, who is going to do the work behind the scenes?

Let's return to the potential customer and his movements and impressions of the restaurant. The building, the sign, and the lighted or unlighted interior are viewable twenty-four hours a day. When the passing traffic views a restaurant which is closed, whatever value there is in seeing neat premises is naturally offset by a disappointment that the restaurant is closed and therefore cannot serve the diner. Then, when the restaurant has opened its doors for business but is seen by the passing traffic without customers, the image is one of an unsuccessful operation. If the personnel are working within the enclosed kitchen, offices, or storage areas, the appearance is the same as if the restaurant were actually closed down. There is no incentive for the passerby to stop and investigate.

THE LOOK OF SUCCESS

Restaurants designed like McDonald's do not therefore present a look of success for a large part of the twenty-four hours of the day when their buildings are viewed by the traffic. Let's estimate the proportion of the twenty-four hours of the day when the restaurant is seen by traffic and during which it will have an unsuccessful look as compared with that proportion of time when it will have a look of success. In an average fast food chain restaurant, the owners may expect to look busy for between four and six hours. If the restaurant has this busy look for six hours at a maximum, then for 25 percent of the twenty-four-hour day the restaurant appears successful while for 75 percent of the time it has an unsuccessful look. In fact, a real peak of traffic sufficient to sustain one of these restaurants might be, in certain cases, for only one or two hours of the day. The rest of the time the restaurant looks like a ghost town.

How often has the reader driven through areas where many restaurants are operating to see one after another of the "giants" where no one is buying? The burger giants take on the appearance of the Kentucky Fried Chicken carry-out stores, which most of the time look as though they are very much in need of business. During these many hours of the day when the operators exhibit an empty dining room in the front part of their buildings, their final hope is that their clerks can be seen, even though through an empty dining room, at their positions at the counter ready to serve the customers. The labor cost goes on continuously; however, the most effective use of employees is when they are in position at the counter to serve food and take cash. One of the most important values of the restaurant operation is the quality and character of the personnel. A good salesclerk can build trade in the worst type of operation; and even in a well-designed restaurant, a salesclerk who cannot be seen is of little value.

These are some of the design weaknesses that are evident in the most successful chain restaurants: (1) placing dining room seating arrangements in front of the carry-out section; and (2) providing places of concealment for employees. These design weaknesses, although they are introduced by the highly successful league leaders, are unwittingly copied by every runner-up just as though they represented the perfect design solution to a restaurant image. Perhaps the number one chain holds its position because of factors other than the design of the building and its interior. Nevertheless, the runners-up make exact copies of the number one operation just to be sure they don't miss.

THE RESTAURANT DRAMA

When a restaurateur plans to build anew or to remodel, he may keep these design weaknesses in mind. If the restaurant operator corrects these weaknesses, he is in a better position to overcome some of the advantages that are inherent in the chain operations.

Before you draw up your plans, take the time to review the present or intended placement of your facilities. If you are planning to locate a kitchen in the rear, consider the possibility of bringing it forward so that the seating areas may be divided to surround the kitchen. In this way, you can give equally speedy attention to all portions of your dining room. When building or remodeling a fast food restaurant, look into the possibilities of creating a kitchen of the open type. If you can provide this, you will add interest to your dining room. It should also attract more diners inasmuch as they can see the employees working in the kitchen through the open glass front of the restaurant. All of this helps to give a look of activity even when there are few or no customers.

Look upon your restaurant as if it were a stage and all the personnel were the actors. That is what they truly are. They are your actors and entertainers who are paid by the hour to perform the services for your customers. They can hardly serve you well in this capacity, however, if they cannot be seen by the customers.

Dress up the ceiling over the kitchen area with a combination of false beams and slanting shingle roof lines. Then provide openings through to the dining rooms so that the heads and shoulders of employees can be seen wherever they are. This increases the dimensions of the room and adds valuable entertainment for the eye. Perhaps the most important factors here are (1) your customers become better acquainted with your personnel and (2) your customers actually help you in the management of the personnel. When the employee knows he is constantly being viewed by the customers, he will limit the amount of time he spends in nonproductive work.

Follow these suggestions in your new building or remodeling program. Review the design of the front of the restaurant as it appears to the passing traffic. Expose more of the interior and of the personnel. Get as much of the action of your restaurant moved as close to the front door as possible. Your front door can be a series of large windows that allow your customers to get quick impressions of the restaurant during the few seconds they are passing by.

PLANNING TIPS

An ideal goal in a plan for a fast food dining room might be described as follows. Provide wide access routes from the street into your parking lot and see that these access routes are well lighted. Then floodlight the building and the sign as well as lighting the sign from within. Plan so that passersby can take in at one quick glance the sight of a few people actually dining and the sight of the personnel moving about and serving. A sales and service counter located near the front door indicates that a guest can get in and out of your restaurant quickly with carry-out foods without having to penetrate into the very center of a large, complex dining room. The location of your counter and food service should speak clearly of service that is fast and separate from larger dining areas.

In fast foods, nothing should appear to delay the ability of your guest to get food in the most uncomplicated and speediest manner, without being subjected to the scrutiny of the sit-down diners. As your potential customer for carry-out foods or your prospective diner is about to drive by your restaurant, he should be sold instantly on the idea of the speedy service and of the simplicity of the manner of providing food to carry out and, in general, of the lack of complications in dealing with you.

In the fast food service, locate your carry-out counter or buffet service unit at a point clearly visible through the windows of the front and two sides of the store. There should be some stand-up dining shelves placed strategically about the front of the store. In this way, those who want to eat while standing up and looking out may do so. In fact, they should be encouraged to do so since they provide a valuable incentive to others to stop and enter the restaurant. They are the first to be seen.

Attractively designed stand-up shelves or window counters can make stand-up dining a popular, if not stylish, thing to do. At the same time, the shelves or counters signal that you are prepared to serve people speedily. They provide a natural look of speed.

In addition to this, it is important to provide booth and bench accommodations designed for two people. Provide these accommodations in the front and at the side of the front of the building where they are always visible through the windows. They should be equipped with the best items of your furniture. One of the benches that form the booths for two persons should extend to form a continuous and longer bench in combination with free-standing tables. When used in this manner, any two or more tables can be pushed together with additional chairs to provide party arrangements. This type of seating should be filled first before you draw the curtains to expose a larger dining space to the rear.

It is good design practice to make clearly defined separations between the stand-up dining shelves in the front windows, a few of the two-seated booths with related continuing benches and pull-up tables, and, finally, the larger main dining room. People do not enjoy being seated in a single, large, square glass-enclosed box in the front part of a restaurant, in clear view of all other people. They feel like goldfish in a glass bowl. Today's seating arrangements should be broken up into smaller more intimate room-like areas. In this case, it's a good idea to use the kitchen itself (preferably an open-type kitchen) as a means of separating the carry-out in the front, with its stand-up dining, from the two-seated booths and the dining space in the rear.

This, then, would allow the operator to supply his kitchen with goods coming in from the outside through the one remaining side wall. This wall, representing the outside of the kitchen, may be one without windows. As such, it provides an excellent place for a sign. Such a sign may be mounted on the side wall itself and floated out from the wall. Lights within can halo each letter against the restaurant building wall.

After building a restaurant in this manner, staff it with employees selected for their personality and neat appearance, and dress them sharply. Then, with a building designed to become a stage for your personnel (the actors), you should go a long way toward overcoming some of the advantages of the larger chain operators.

Index

THE CONSCIENCE OF THE RICH NATIONS:

The Development Assistance Committee
and the Common Aid Effort

THE CONSCIENCE OF
THE RICH NATIONS:

The Development Assistance Committee
and the Common Aid Effort

by SEYMOUR J. RUBIN

Published for the
Council on Foreign Relations
by
Harper & Row, Publishers
New York and London

The Council on Foreign Relations is a nonprofit institution devoted to the study of political, economic, and strategic problems as related to American foreign policy. It takes no stand, expressed or implied, on American policy.

The authors of books published under the auspices of the Council are responsible for their statements of fact and expressions of opinion. The Council is responsible only for determining that they should be presented to the public.

For a list of Council publications see pages 162-164.

To J.B.R.

IN MEMORY OF EDWARD JOHN NOBLE

The Policy Book series of the Council on Foreign Relations is published under a grant from the Edward John Noble Foundation in memory of Mr. Noble and his interest in encouraging American leadership.

Policy Books of the Council on Foreign Relations

It has been said again and again that the world's greatest problem in the decades ahead is the gap between the rich nations and the poor nations. Whether it will be met, in ways that are not totally disruptive of world order, will depend largely on the governments and peoples of the developed parts of the world—on their "conscience," their specific policies and aid programs, and their ability to work with each other no less than with the underdeveloped nations.

A little known and relatively modest chapter in this story is the effort already made to coordinate Western aid policies which has centered in the Development Assistance Committee. It is an important chapter, however, one which shows what has and has not been done, and which also throws light on what can and should be done. The United States, as the largest provider of aid, has had a leading role both in the establishment and in the continuing work of the Committee, which has had an American chairman from the start.

This is the tenth in the series of Policy Books of the Council on Foreign Relations. These books have a twofold purpose: first, to provide readers in this country and elsewhere with essays and analytical studies of the highest quality on problems of world significance; and second, to contribute to constructive thinking on American policies of the future. They are deliberately kept brief, not with the aim of simplification but to present with a minimum of factual background and detail the reasoned conclusions of individual authors with special experience and qualifications.

The Council was fortunate in persuading Seymour J. Rubin to write this book. Mr. Rubin has had long experience, both inside and outside the government, in international economic affairs. He served as United States Representative on the Development Assistance Committee from 1962 to 1964, a critical period of its existence. He is, accordingly, in a unique position to discuss the Committee's record and also the broader questions of policy concerning the relations of the Western nations, among themselves and with the less developed nations, which give meaning to its successes and its failures.

This is Mr. Rubin's book. The views are his own, not those of the Council or of the review group which was formed to discuss his manuscript with him. The Council takes responsibility for the decision to publish it, believing it to be a significant contribution to thought on a problem which will grow in its dimensions and in urgency during the years ahead.

JOHN C. CAMPBELL
Editor

By Way of Acknowledgment

In the writing of this book, I have been assisted by the many persons with whom, over the course of several years, I have discussed ideas or problems mentioned in its pages. I owe a debt to the many writers on aid, foreign policy, the national interest, and the permutations thereof, especially the work of Asher, Black, Coffin, Feis, Galbraith, Mason, Montgomery, Staley, and others. I have used extensively the published materials of the Secretariat of the Organization for Economic Cooperation and Development, the annual reports of the two chairmen until now of the Development Assistance Committee, James W. Riddleberger and Willard L. Thorp. A study by Dr. Goran Ohlin of the OECD Development Center has been helpful.

I also have pondered the comments made to me by the distinguished group of experts assembled to review the manuscript under the aegis of the Council on Foreign Relations. Some, if not all, of their cogent comments are reflected in the text. Included in the group were Robert E. Asher, Henry G. Aubrey, Harold van B. Cleveland, William Diebold, Jr., Deane R. Hinton, Albert O. Hirschman, Jacob J. Kaplan, Edward S. Lynch, Carl Marcy, Richard B. Palmer, Gardner Patterson, Jo W. Saxe, and Mrs. Helena Stalson. Emilio Collado, Richard Demuth, Paul Hoffman, and Michael L. Hoffman, though not present for the general discussion, made valued suggestions. The genial incisiveness of the chairman of the group, Raymond Vernon, set the tone for a vigorous and useful exchange of views.

It remains to be said that what appears in the following pages results not only from these impeccable sources, but also from my own experience in and around the Development Assistance Committee, my talks with those conversant with one or another aspect of the subject, and from my own cogitations. I have taken literally the suggestion of the Council on Foreign Relations that I write a "personal" book. That much I can honestly claim to have done, without diminishing my acknowledgment of gratitude.

SEYMOUR J. RUBIN

Washington, D.C.
February 1965

Contents

Chapter I

The Common Aid Effort

> The belief in the material progress of mankind is
> not old. During the greater part of history such a
> belief was neither compatible with experience nor en-
> couraged by religion.
>
> JOHN MAYNARD KEYNES

The occasion is, these days, a usual one. Another meeting of an
international organization is about to take place. This one, the
Development Assistance Committee of the Organization for
Economic Cooperation and Development, meets in Paris at
the Château de la Muette. The Château is not the usual sanitized
and characterless public building; it was formerly a home of the
Rothschilds, then of the Organization for European Economic
Cooperation of the Marshall Plan days, is now the headquarters
of the OECD, successor to the OEEC. The change marks the
success of the Marshall Plan and is testimony to the various
European "economic miracles" of the past fifteen years.

The room is large, with windows that run from floor to ceiling, open onto a flagstone terrace, and look toward a well-
groomed lawn. Beyond, one hears the murmur of Paris traffic,

quieted now these several years by a surprisingly effective ban on auto horns. Inside is the U-shaped table which is the mark of the international meeting, the rows of chairs at its exterior, the name signs of the countries represented, the small interior table for the lesser functionaries of the Secretariat. At the head of the table, at the center of the crossbar of the U, is the card for the chairman. Flanked by the officials of the Secretariat, microphone before him, earphones for the simultaneous translation at the ready, he faces, at the far end of the room, a series of glassed-in enclosures, more box than room, from which the translators view indifferently the arriving delegates.

The weak sunshine of Paris filters through the windows as the delegates arrive. There is a quiet bustle of chairs being pulled back, of words of recognition and greeting, of muted conversation as one delegate or another mutters a few words of comment or persuasion to his colleague, or confers hastily with a Secretariat member. Some ten minutes after the hour for which the meeting has been set, the chairman looks about, clears his throat, rings a small bell, and delegates settle into their chairs, light cigarettes, and wait for his opening remarks.

With appropriate geographic variations, the scene could be almost endlessly repeated the world over—in the meetings of various committees of the United Nations in New York or Geneva; in the meetings of a proliferating number of committees, within or outside the UN system, in Rome or Santiago or Lagos or Cairo. The international meeting has become a feature of the life of governments and private organizations. Resident delegations are established not only in capitals, not merely at the seat of the United Nations, but also at the headquarters of organizations which are regional or functional. All spawn an incessant series of meetings. Officials of governments fly halfway round the world for a two-day session in Bangkok or Washington, and exchange tips on the good and the bad of hotels, restaurants, airlines. Of the making of committees, particularly study committees, there is no end. A glance at the pages of the current Department of State *Bulletin* will show American officials in attendance at conference sessions from one end of the world to another, in forums as genial as those concerned with tourism and as difficult as those concerned with disarmament. The topics are as varied as the activities of the human race.

The DAC and Bilateral Aid

Why, therefore, devote an essay to the problems of one more organization, and a little known one at that—the Development Assistance Committee? The DAC is small, consisting of fifteen members only.[1] It is a part of another, larger, and therefore presumably more important organization, the OECD. It rarely publicizes its meetings, and when it does, its feeble attempt to obtain some of the news spotlight is more often than not greeted with the massive indifference of all but the most comprehensive or specialized segments of the press. It does not have the interest of being at the center of visible controversy—neither the East-West strife of a Security Council session nor the clash of divergent Western policies at a meeting of NATO or the European Economic Community.

But, for all its quietness and obscurity, the DAC is not without interest and importance. Interest derives from the fact that it deals with a subject which, unlike the organization itself, is at

[1] The members as of mid-1965 were Austria, Belgium, Canada, Denmark, France, the Federal Republic of Germany, Italy, Japan, the Netherlands, Norway, Portugal, the United Kingdom, the United States, and the Commission of the European Economic Community. Sweden became a member in July 1965 and, as of the time of writing, has not yet participated substantively in the work of the DAC.

the very center of national and international political relations: foreign aid, or, more broadly speaking, the place of aid in the relationship between the richer and the poorer nations of the world. Importance derives from the fact that the DAC, whatever its present shortcomings or accomplishments, is probably the leading forum of the richer nations for discussing their mutual interests involved in the policies, administration, and effectiveness of aid.

The Development Assistance Committee is obviously not alone in this role. Although for historical as well as substantive reasons it dwells a little apart, the DAC is a component body of the larger Organization for Economic Cooperation and Development and draws on its Secretariat. Within the Château de la Muette there are other sections of the OECD whose work bears importantly on aid: the Trade Committee for example, or the committees which handle questions as relevant to aid policy as international monetary liquidity or rates of growth. A variety of institutional arrangements in the OECD cut across the organization lines of the DAC; for example, the OECD is itself a donor of technical assistance. The Development Center of the OECD, formed in 1963, has assembled scholars and researchers, has conducted seminars, and has participated in meetings of the DAC. The DAC is, thus, far from isolated.

From these others, however, the DAC is different not merely in the amount of time which it gives to the issue of mutuality of aid interests but in the tone of its activities. The DAC is a standing committee, with a permanent resident chairman; its meetings, its working groups, are in continuing session except during the quiet Paris August. Representatives from capitals arrive frequently to participate in its deliberations, and the informal corridor discussions between delegates provide a nexus between more formal meetings. In this exchange of views and discussion, it is its theme that gives the DAC its tone: What should, and what can, the developed nations do to increase the flow of development assistance and to improve the quality of that flow? What can be done, by way of better cooperation between donors, to obtain an over-all aid effort which will facilitate achievement of the common aims of the donors? It is here, obviously, that the substantive problems of definition arise, for the content of such coordination as may be accomplished depends on the extent to which the aims of donors, as well as their motives, are in fact mutual.

The DAC operates in the knowledge that the broad motives and aims of the donors are, if not identical, at least compatible. All seek to promote free societies and rising standards of living in the developing nations. But each has also special interests of various sorts. It is this combination of mutuality and difference, of divergence within the bounds of fundamental agreement, that makes the DAC an organization that is defining its task as it performs it. It is this push and pull of forces that shape the concepts, that give meaning to the words of the resolutions and to the speeches about progress and cooperation.

The DAC exists in a vortex, but it is no passive object. It has a force of its own, something more than the mere totaling of its fifteen members. That force results from the fact that, in a variety of meetings, conversations, and talks, it gives its attention always to the matter of coordinating the aid aspects of the foreign policies of the free world. The members consult each other on their aid programs, with the intermediate objective of harmonizing policies and procedures, and the ultimate objective of making aid a more efficient tool of the broadly agreed aims of their separate foreign policies.

In most, if not all, of the donor states criticism of aid has increased in recent years—criticism based largely upon dissatisfaction with the results.[2] In the United States many are critical of recent aid programs although they remain supporters of the role of aid both in American foreign policy and in the relations of the developed nations of the free world to the less developed nations. On grounds of increased effectiveness, they have sometimes advocated a multilateral approach: assigning more of the responsibility for development loans and grants to international agencies, which presumably can act free of the political pressures which influence national administration.

Despite pressures to increase the flow of resources to the multilateral agencies which make aid funds and technical assistance available, the bulk of assistance from developed to less developed countries is "bilateral." Far more American aid to Viet-Nam or Brazil, to Nigeria or India, is likely to flow through the United States Agency for International Development (AID) than through contributions to the International Bank for Reconstruction and Development (IBRD, or World Bank), the Inter-American Development Bank, or the Special Fund of the United Nations. Similarly, the bulk of British aid is directed by the Commonwealth Relations Office, the Treasury, or the new Ministry for Overseas Development; French aid goes via a variety of French ministries and agencies; German aid is coordinated by Bonn's Ministry of Economic Cooperation; and similarly for the others.

The 1964 Report of the Chairman of the Development Assistance Committee stated that "in 1963 total official bilateral net disbursements reached the level of $5,679 million" and that "in 1963 the net official multilateral contribution dropped to $296

2 In the pages which follow, such terms as "donor" and "recipient" are used as convenient labels, and are not intended to denote more than the generally accepted classification of "developed" and "developing" states. It is recognized that the categories are vague, that those who receive may give more than those who donate, and that many states are in both categories. The context should make the sense clear in each case.

million."[3] The quoted statement exaggerates the comparative importance of bilateral aid, since it refers only to new commitments to multilateral agencies which may well vary greatly from year to year. The 1964 commitments of aid by the multilateral organizations were around $1.6 billion; disbursements in the same year were $927 million. Nor do the figures given in the 1964 Report include the already available resources of the international institutions; and new international commitments (for example, to the International Development Association and the Inter-American Development Bank) have been made or are on the horizon.[4] In fact, the multilateral outflow has grown faster than has the bilateral. Nevertheless, the great bulk of the flow of assistance as it exists at present is bilateral.

I suggest that it will remain so. Foreign policy, including aid policy, is based on the national interest of each donor. Decisions as to size and allocation of an aid policy depend on each state's appraisal of that interest. Since the interests of different states are far from coterminous, even when they include broadly similar views and purposes, the retention of national control over the bulk of aid is natural, or at least rational. Even when objectives coincide, as for example when all agree on a program of assistance to a specified recipient, each donor is likely to favor its own methods, its own commercial or political policies, and seeks to relate its aid to these aspects of its relationship with the receiving nation.

The question may legitimately be put whether in this state

[3] The 1965 Report stated that, based on preliminary estimates, the total official net bilateral disbursements in 1964 were $5,554 million; official payments to multilateral agencies by DAC members were $367 million net. The 1965 Report also pointed out that private capital outflows increased in 1964, more than offsetting the drop in official bilateral aid flows. See Appendix Table.

[4] For example, for a variety of reasons, the United States has proposed a cooperative $1 billion development program for Southeast Asia and, within that, has offered a $200-million subscription to the Asian Development Bank, with another $100 million to go into a special multilateral loan fund.

of affairs there is substance in an organization which stands for a "common effort." Where, other than in the phrases which as often cloud as clarify a policy, is there the mutuality of motive, of objective, or of technique which would seem necessary to such an effort?

So far as purpose is concerned, there is little public dispute as to the broad objectives of aid. All would and do agree with the statement of U.S. policy contained in the Act for International Development of 1961:

> It is declared to be the policy of the United States to aid the efforts of the peoples of economically underdeveloped areas to develop their resources and improve their living and working conditions by encouraging the exchange of technical knowledge and skill and the flow of investment capital to countries which provide conditions under which such technical assistance and capital can effectively and constructively contribute to raising standards of living, creating new sources of wealth, increasing productivity, and expanding productive power.[5]

Statements of other governments are as breathtakingly sweeping —and as commendable. The style may differ, from the rolling periods in which a De Gaulle "press conference" is staged, to the restrained phrases of a British White Paper, to the dreary prose of the usual official declaration of high aspiration. But, whatever the manner in which the sentiment is expressed, all agree that the objective is noble as well as useful and that the self-interest of the donor is enlightened. It follows that cooperation is a virtue not only in itself but in speeding the attainment of a worthy goal.

It will be increasingly important to harmonize the bilateral aid programs. The existence of multiple donors makes comparison inevitable. At home and abroad, the aid actions of donors interact. The effort to increase amounts of aid and to improve

[5] P.L. 87-195 (1961).

the terms of development loans relies on a similarity of actions by those similarly situated. The coordination of the bilateral programs of aid thus becomes crucial not only to effectiveness and efficiency but also to the antecedent questions of the size, the scope, and the nature of aid programs.

Coordination holds out the happy prospect of achieving the virtues of multilateral, internationalized action, without the pain of relinquishing charge of one's resources. Whether this prospect is in fact realizable, or to what extent, is a serious question—the main subject of these pages.

Much can be done through consultation and discussion. What lies behind and beyond consultation—joint conclusions and agreed actions—raises questions which stem from the very nature of bilateral aid, that is, its close identification with national policy and its function as an arm of that policy. For this reason, the substantive content of the word "coordination" is more likely to be found in what governments do than in what they say. And as aid policies evolve, mature, and increasingly interlock, the variety of ways in which practice defines the concept is certain to take on new and greater significance. At the least, coordination now means an attempt by the bilateral donors to face together the problems of size, scope, and nature of aid in the context of an agreed effort to improve standards of living in the less developed world. At the most, it might mean a merging of policies and programs far beyond what now exists.

Other considerations, directed toward public and legislative support, reinforce the case for cooperation. It should make the joint aid effort more effective. Additionally, emphasis on a co-ordinated program buttresses the individual, bilateral programs of aid against the attacks to which each of them is subjected at home. Of late, there have been reminders in several other donor nations that aid long continued brings with it the same problems of public and legislative support so familiar to the United States. In the United States discontent with the continuing size and scope of foreign aid is thought to be somewhat mitigated by pointing out that others—those foreigners whose hardheadedness is grudgingly admired and contrasted with our own less realistic policy—also participate in a foreign aid effort which, in proportion to their resources, is sometimes greater than that of the United States. As a consequence, the AID presentation to the Congress for fiscal year 1966 stresses that a substantial effort is in fact made by the other "Western" (a word which for this purpose includes Japan) developed powers, that these various aid programs are, in one way or another, harmonized, and that in "fiscal year 1966, 85 per cent of all AID development loans in Asia and Africa will be committed through these multi-national consortia or consultative groups."[6]

The size of this percentage figure of "coordinated" aid, however, permits some skepticism, which is centered on the threshold questions: In this context what is the meaning of coordination? What consequences flow from the consensus of donors (and recipients too) as to the merit of coordination? What is the significance of the assertion that the great bulk of American aid is "committed through" consortia or consultative groups?

At the outset, I suggest that "coordination" has at least two main dimensions: the extent to which donor nations will harmonize the size and the nature of their aid programs; and the extent to which they will bring into compatibility the manner in which they conduct their aid operations. One might postulate a coordination which only touched operations: given several programs, each contributing funds or technical assistance to a single recipient, the sole issue would then be methods of avoiding

6 Summary Presentation to the Congress; Proposed Mutual Defense and Development Programs, March 1965, p. 14.

conflicts and of meshing the activities of the several donors so as to maximize results. But in the sense in which the term is used by the DAC, and indeed by most proponents of "coordination," it connotes a mutuality antecedent to operations: Should there be an agreed level of aid? If so, how should it be judged? What kind of aid should this be—capital or technical assistance, loans or grants, hard or soft credits?

The DAC, in its process of defining by doing, has taken coordination to lie in both of these areas. The essential fact of the DAC's existence is that it starts with a commitment of members *both* to an increased and improved aid effort *and* to harmonization of aid policies and procedures. The distinction between the two commitments should not be overemphasized; rightly, it is often ignored in the work of the DAC. Without some working together, the several bilateral programs lose effectiveness; this, in turn, reacts badly against those who seek aid appropriations. But it is a distinction, nevertheless, of substantial importance to an understanding of what is comprehended within the phrase, so recurrent in DAC dialogue, "the common aid effort."

What the DAC has done and can do in defining and achieving coordination is the inquiry of this book. In describing and analyzing the workings of the organization, its problems, successes and failures, its purposes, prospects and techniques, one may derive some conclusions not merely about the organization but also, more importantly, about the probable future of the common aid effort.

I have left to one side, in these pages, such problems as those of the transfer of resources by way of private capital investments and even such weighty and substantive issues of foreign aid as its failures and achievements, its deficiencies and virtues. Many books, articles, and reports are available to the student of these matters. Here, except to the extent that the broader issues are clearly relevant to a fair inquiry into the avowed cooperative attempt of governments to improve their aid efforts, I have limited my attention to official aid, and to the question of the realities of, and the prospects for, the common aid effort and its apostle, the Development Assistance Committee.

Ways of Coordinating Aid

The tightest and neatest form of coordination is that achieved by national contributions to international entities which themselves administer aid: the World Bank or its soft-loan affiliate, the International Development Association, or the Inter-American Development Bank, or the newly combined United Nations Special Fund and Expanded Program of Technical Assistance.[7] Here the possibility of conflict *within* the organization of course exists. The executive directors of the banks or the administrators of the UN entities may have different views as to the best application of their available funds. But once the financial contributions of members are made, the decision as to use is reached by the internal mechanisms of these organizations. National differences of opinion are eventually reconciled, of necessity, within these decision-making processes.

Thus the pooling of funds under a single administration—for example, that of the World Bank or the UN Special Fund—is in a very real sense the ultimate in coordination. A substantial part of a donor's ability to control the direction and use of his aid is lost when the national decision to make the contribution is taken. Various devices, such as weighted voting, may represent a continuing string on those funds. Even so, common administration of an organization with irrevocably committed resources

---

[7] I do not speak here of the coordinative arrangements, or lack thereof, between the international organizations themselves.

means that conflicting national interests are subordinated to the agreed objectives of the organization, as interpreted by its executive. Where the executive is strong, as it is in the World Bank, the coordinative effect is increased. (This high degree of coordination with its consequent loss of national control is, conversely, the reason why the proportion of aid from developed countries which flows through the international agencies is relatively small.)

A second form of coordination is that of the consortium. Here, again, a rather high degree of cooperation and harmonization can be achieved. The stated objective of the consortium is to bring together a group of donors for the purpose of furthering the economic development of a particular recipient. The technique is to study the needs and the possibilities of the recipient, to arrive at a conclusion about the scope and nature of the external assistance which ought to be made available,[8] and then to proceed to a fund-raising exercise in which each of the donors is asked what it will contribute and how the contribution will be made. At various stages consultations are held with the recipient, directed toward a better understanding of what are the requirements, what progress has been made, what has been the use of domestic resources, and so forth. At the least, the procedure enables the recipient to avoid going through separate explanations for each potential donor. At best, it can achieve very much more for both recipient and donors.

Since the consortium concentrates on a single developing country, and by definition is composed of donor countries which have both a substantial interest and an implied willingness to contribute, a considerable degree of consensus is likely. Consensus is the more possible because the consortium is generally

---

[8] More explicitly, the resources necessary and available to fill the foreign exchange gap in a one-year segment of a multiyear development plan.

assisted by expert staff, who have consulted extensively with the planners and officials of the recipient. Harmonization of programs, however, is limited: contributions, though "within" the consortium framework, are bilateral, worked out by each donor and the recipient under arrangements which are subject to the delays, conditions, and general requirements of bilateral aid agreements; and the attitudes of donors reflect not only mutual objectives but their ever-present commercial and economic, if not political, differences.

Consortia have been formed to provide funds for India and Pakistan under the leadership of the World Bank, and for Greece and Turkey under the aegis of the Organization for Economic Cooperation and Development. Of the latter two, only that for Turkey has had much substance, since it has been the unmistakable if largely unstated assumption in the OECD that the Greek need for external assistance is at this late date limited and special and can be handled by loans from various international lending entities or from individual donors, largely on conventional terms.[9] The Indian and Pakistan consortia, on the other hand, have been and are active and useful in stating requirements, in following development progress, and in achieving international cooperation both among the donors and between donors and recipient.[10] The Turkish consortium, after some initial rough sailing, has also made contributions both in providing funds for use within a development plan and in bringing about an essential readjustment of the crushing burden of Turkey's external debt.[11]

[9] In 1965 the Greek consortium became more active than it had previously been.

[10] The 1965 border crisis and the consequent reluctance of the donors (particularly the United States) to make firm their pledges have undoubtedly affected the capabilities of the consortia.

[11] See Chapter IV, footnote 15.

The consultative group is a device to bring together donors in the kind of mutual consultation which characterizes the consortium, but without its fund-raising. It is likely that members do in fact expect their interest to be expressed financially as well as intellectually, but the commitment, if it exists at all, is vaguer by far than that implied by membership in a consortium. This fact is sufficiently cogent so that consultative groups have supplanted consortia in the favor of donors, and several have now come into existence, mostly under the sponsorship of the World Bank, including a group for Thailand formed in 1965. The techniques of examining the economy of the developing nation, of consulting with its officials, and of attempting to arrive at common conclusions about steps necessary for its development, are much the same as those of a full-fledged consortium. Vigorous leadership is essential to the success of the consortium or consultative group.

For Latin America, the Inter-American Development Bank has provided a strong initiative. In 1965 it began what may be the first of a series of ventures into the technique of the consultative group by organizing one for Ecuador. This brought together representatives of nineteen nations for a three-day meeting, which resulted in an announcement of "expressed interest" in financing forty projects within Ecuador's ten-year economic and social development plan, with a total cost of $340.3 million, including external requirements to the amount of $173 million.[12] The device of the consultative group, under the aegis of the World Bank or the Inter-American Development Bank, perhaps under the sponsorship of new regional banks as they begin operations, seems likely to be utilized frequently.

[12] Financiers have always had trouble in finding a way to say that they might, or probably will, or think that they possibly could, make a commitment. The "expressed interest" phraseology is difficult to analyze; it is probably akin to the "sympathetic consideration" of diplomats.

The coordination which exists within consortia or consultative groups—and a fortiori within a multilateral organization—is likely to have an appreciable effect on the aid policies of donors. It encourages agreement on development goals and progress toward their attainment. More doubtful is the effect of coordination when it is not, as is the consortium, focused on a single recipient. An example is the Colombo Plan.

This is an association mainly of members of the British Commonwealth, some neighboring states in the Far East and South Asia, and the United States, and takes its name from the fact that it was formed in 1950 at Colombo, Ceylon. Its purpose is cooperation for development. That cooperation may well have both economic and political significance, but it is quite clearly limited and special. India is, for example, in the Colombo Plan area; but the World Bank and the consortium, not the Plan, are the substantive vehicles of coordinating aid to India.

The Colombo Plan holds annual meetings. The formula for these meetings involves a two-stage procedure: first, a meeting of "officials," at which there is a confrontation, an exchange of views, and a discussion of problems at the "working level," and second, a ministerial meeting immediately following. Both official and ministerial sessions are characterized by a great deal of useful fraternizing and by numerous bilateral discussions between the government officials of the developed and the developing member nations. The chief impression, taken from the ministerial meeting at least, is one of formal, predictable speeches. In these speeches the less developed nations emphasize their great needs, the contribution made over the years by their resources to the prosperity of the developed, and the desirability of increasing the flow of aid, of making repayment easier, and of lowering the barriers to their exports. On the other side, the speeches will be less forthcoming, and are likely to recount contributions already made, projects recently started or completed, and to take a confident view of the future, given a reasonable degree of international tranquillity. During the Bangkok meeting of 1963 an effort, repeated at London in 1964, was made to stimulate discussion rather than set speeches. Though the attempt was reasonably successful, it hardly revolutionized the methodology or the purposes of the Colombo Plan.

In this context coordination obviously has a different definition than it does, for example, in a pledging session of a consortium. "Coordination" under the Colombo Plan means that all concerned concur in the broad and general objective of economic and social development, and that they are prepared, in the meetings of "officials," to discuss programs. In specifics, it means that they are prepared to pool a limited amount of resources in the field of technical assistance, and to discuss their capital and technical assistance requirements or availabilities. It does not mean a serious and sustained attempt at analyzing aid problems or reconciling programs, or a joint effort to resolve major difficulties.

To say that the aid programs of the donor countries are coordinated may thus mean much or little. At the one extreme, they may have contributed their funds to the control of a common administrator; at the other, they may all merely subscribe to generally acceptable principles, sometimes within the tranquil context of an association like the Colombo Plan. Coordination may mean an attempt by donors in a consortium to make a joint assessment of needs and a joint attempt to fill these needs. It may mean that donors and recipients come together in a common effort. That effort, however, may itself vary from the close, exacting examination of country plans and requirements of the Alliance for Progress to the butterfly touch of review under the Colombo Plan.

In this broad spectrum of methods for achieving cooperation and coordination, and beginning with the premise of bilateral (that is to say, national) aid programs, the Development Assistance Committee occupies both a middle and a distinctive place.

A consortium starts with the task of helping in the economic development of a selected beneficiary. It tests deeply its members' will toward cooperation, but within a narrowly limited area. Those who enter are already committed to assistance in a specific and highly visible context. The consultative group has many of the same characteristics. Although the commitment to provide funds is less definite, it also functions on an *ad hoc* basis, with participation being an acknowledgment of a particularized interest in a specific less developed country.

The Development Assistance Committee, on the other hand, has built its house on the foundation of the general will of members to cooperate not in a consultative group or consortium for a single country but wherever the aid programs of the free-world donors function and meet. Its techniques are designed both to probe and to extend this will—to ask whether the practice of the donors reflects their statement of principle, and to suggest ways in which practice can better confirm the principle. In the consortium and other devices, specified development targets are the objective. Coordination among the donors is an avenue leading toward that objective. With the DAC, emphasis is on the means as much as on the end. The task is to pave the avenue, in the hope and expectation that to do so will speed up and make easier the attainment of the development objective.

Whatever the specific topic in the Château de la Muette when the DAC meets, the discussion is thus, in a sense, procedural. In this same sense, it is a step or two removed from the scene of development action. As in most coordinative sessions, the delegates are likely to be home-office types, desk-bound for the most part

—the coordinators and administrators from Bonn or London or Washington, not the back-country fellows who get out where the projects are and feel the dirt in their hands. The excitement and feeling of accomplishment that arise from projects planned, built, completed, and seen are absent, being replaced by reports on administration and on programs, by statistics of debt and of aid, by analyses of methods and of recurrent problems. There is not likely to be the specificity of the appraisal and fund-raising exercise of a consortium meeting. DAC conversations are likely to make heads nod as the Paris day drones on, and as the shadows lengthen delegates may surreptitiously consult their watches. But if the excitement of imminent action is lacking, there is nevertheless a genuine sense of relevance and of importance.

What the DAC does, more regularly and more explicitly than the other means of bringing together those interested in development aid, is to explore, define, and extend the content of the "common aid effort" of the free-world donors. It begins with a sense of conscience—that aid is an obligation of the society of free-world developed nations. It continues with the day-by-day attempt to put substance into the sometimes glittering, sometimes pallid, generalities—to see, case by case, what nations consider to be their commitment in fact to an increased and improved flow of aid, and to coordination in the interest of effectiveness.

Since, despite real and inevitable divergences, the broad interests of the DAC members do agree, considerable progress has been made. Since the problems of development, and of the role of aid in development, are difficult, and since the several programs of the donors respond to a variety of motives, not all of which are compatible, that progress has been far from spectacular.

The DAC deals always with the line at which the edge of one donor's program is in contact with that of another, with problems that are common to nations which have increasingly made aid a part of their national long-range policy. It is at this point of contact that the easy slogans are tested against the hard realities, and where cooperation in action will—or will not—be achieved. It is the continuing nature of the DAC effort to achieve accord, and the continual testing of the substance of each member's stated adherence to the principles of improvement and coopera- tion, that gives the DAC a unique place in the congeries of international groupings which deal with aid to the less developed nations of the world.

Chapter II

The Programs of Aid

Because of what we call it, and because of how it has been administered, and because it is far away, we don't realize that this investment is not only one of the most Christian acts that this great, powerful rich country could do, but is an act of necessity if we are to preserve our image in the world and, most of all, our society. . . . No President . . . can fail to extend the hand and heart of the country to those who are struggling elsewhere.

PRESIDENT LYNDON B. JOHNSON, April 21, 1964

The aid program of each of the donor nations, minor as well as major, bears a resemblance to the programs of others; but the divergences are often as marked as the similarities. In the Development Assistance Committee the developed nations of the free world have expressed their commitment to cooperate with each other in the achievement of the common objectives of their programs. Because a flood of rhetoric overlays most statements of foreign policy, an inquiry into mutuality of objectives must begin by asking what are the actualities of each of these programs, how they correspond and how they differ.

The differences, in many cases, may be in administration, in methodology, in national temperament or natural resources—that which makes it more likely for Norway to export skills than capital, and to operate on a small scale, while the United States can move through a series of grandiose programs from Marshall Plan to Alliance for Progress with an ease that, depending on one's point of view, excites enthusiastic praise or bitter blame for the persistent continuity of American grants and loans. But differences may also result from diverging appraisals of national interests or of foreign possibilities. The similarity or conflict of objectives in respect of their aid programs is the most important determinant of both the will and ability of the members of the DAC to achieve harmonization of policies and procedures.

Capital exports to less developed countries are not a new phenomenon. Prior to the First World War British and French capital went to these countries in large volume, more than comparable in relation to gross national income to the present flow of resources from the developed to the less developed areas. Nevertheless, it is only since World War II that nations have to any great extent faced the problems of administering official aid funds. Prewar investment went where, from the point of view of the investor, it could bring the best return. Economic benefit to the less developed country was a frequent, and sometimes necessary, concomitant; but it was not the avowed *raison d'être,* as it is now, of large-scale, official aid. It was only in the 1950s that substantial public funds and technical assistance were first directed toward the less developed countries as part of a deliberate, long-range attempt to foster their economic development, and to influence the relations between the developed and less developed halves of the world.

Arrival of so many new nations on the diplomatic scene has been matched by an almost mushroomlike proliferation of development programs. The provision of aid has responded to needs, generally urgent in nature, not to deliberate and detailed policy planning. At first the assistance extended by the United States, the principal postwar source of help, sought to provide relief and rehabilitation through an international organization, the United Nations Relief and Rehabilitation Administration, and to promote recovery through the national-international techniques of the Marshall Plan. Programs were then hastily devised for countries actually or potentially under attack—for Greece and Turkey, for Korea, for Viet-Nam. The smaller programs of other donors have similarly responded to specific felt needs, not to a planned attack on the problems of underdevelopment. Though all the programs had economic (and social) objectives and implications, it was only with the development aid provided in the 1950s that the growth and progress of the less developed nations were made an important if not essential objective of the policy of the developed nations. Aid thus became something more than the response to urgent crisis, or the correlative of a special political relationship.

In the United States, thinking directed toward a general theory of aid was amply available prior to the presidential election of 1960.[1] But the writings of scholars attained status with the

---

[1] There has been, surprisingly, little and tardy analysis of an interesting if collateral aspect of large-scale foreign aid—its impact on the domestic distribution of political power. It is evident, for example, that when an important part of American foreign policy depends on the appropriation, annually, of large sums of money by the Congress, the power to determine the conduct of foreign affairs will pass in part from the executive to the legislative branch of government. Similarly, the House of Representatives will absorb some authority from the Senate, since legislation rather than appointments and treaties is the vital core of aid. The long Senate-House conference on the foreign aid legislation of 1965, and the eventual triumph of the once lowly regarded House Foreign Affairs Committee, illustrates the point. To some extent, other donors also are finding that aid appropriations are a vehicle for increased legislative participation in foreign affairs.

designation by President-elect Kennedy, in the fall of 1960, of a special task force on aid, which based its recommendations for reorganization of the aid program and agency on the plausible theory that progress in all the developing nations was a long-term, important interest of the United States. If this proposition holds true for the United States, it would seem equally relevant to other developed "Western" nations. But the proposition is not self-evident: aid in the policy of the European donors, for example, has been based on traditional relationships more than on general development theory or global policy. Discussion of principle, of a broad thesis about aid, seems somewhat irrelevant to programs which are on the one side an *ad hoc* response to crisis and on the other the natural product of long history.

Central to a discussion of either the possibilities or the merits of coordination is the issue of motivation. What is it that now, if not previously, leads a nation to its decisions on aid? What do donors expect from their aid expenditures—economic development, social progress, better political relations, preservation of positions of favor or advantage, or a mélange of results?

Some conforming of techniques, some reduction or elimination of operational divergence, is possible between differently motivated programs even if they seek different—but not conflicting—objectives. But the extent to which a truthfully "common" aid effort can be achieved largely depends on motive and on objective. Since what nations, like people, intend can better be found in what they do than in what they say about what they do, a brief examination of the bilateral programs of aid follows.[2]

2 It need hardly be added that motives can change, purposes shift, and that the DAC is designed to facilitate the exchange of views which may lead to a new outlook.

The United States Program

The United States initiated modern, large-scale peacetime aid and maintains by far the largest, most extensive, and most explained aid program in the world. Uncounted words have been written and spoken, not only about the manner in which the program is carried out and the results which have been achieved, but also about the motives behind it. Nonetheless, a consensus has hardly been attained.

Statements of motive vary, at least in their emphasis, according to time and circumstances. Official explanations of the program are addressed to audiences as different as the House Appropriations Committee, the National Council of Churches, or the peoples of Bolivia or Burma. The different interests of these groups themselves are indicative of the main substantive reason for lack of agreement on the why of aid.

The United States program is one which partakes of many motives and seeks various objectives. Many of these are consistent; some may not be. The program, being above all pragmatic, changes its emphases, its motivations, and, all too often, its administration. Even if one puts to one side its military and quasi-military aspects, the development assistance effort of the United States covers projects as various as schooling in the Andes and dams in Turkey. It makes some loans at next-to-commercial rates and others on terms so easy that they are in substance semigrants. In seeking development, it extends its hand to democracies and to dictatorships in the Western Hemisphere and to states which are each other's enemies in the Middle East or the Asian subcontinent. In these circumstances a unitary theory or a single dominant motive is indeed, for obvious and valid reasons, difficult to formulate.

However understandable the absence of a single rationale for

aid may be, the size of the program, the number of its beneficiaries, and the spotty results have occasioned recurrent demands,
many of them originating in the Congress, for reappraisal and
re-evaluation. In accordance with the American genius, this out-
cry has brought about, in administration after administration,
the appointment of committees, generally composed of distinguished private citizens, to do this task.

Some of the problems of stating an American motive for aid
are evident from the title of the group, under the chairmanship
of General Lucius Clay, which President Kennedy named to
make a study in 1963—the Committee to Strengthen the Security
of the Free World. Rightly or wrongly, the title was taken, at
least abroad, as suggesting that American aid was dominantly a
function of the cold war and that the humanitarian motives of
the Truman Point Four proposals were of slight significance in
the *Realpolitik* of the 1960s. The report itself did little to counter
that impression. It started by emphasizing that "Each of our
Presidents since foreign aid began has repeatedly expressed his
judgment that this assistance is essential to the national interests
of the United States . . ."[3] Though it could be otherwise con-
strued, the phraseology implied that a disinterested desire to see
improvement in the standards of living of the impoverished was
a minor and subordinate reason for American aid.

To rest aid on the national interest is natural; but to do so is
only to begin the task of definition. The case may be made that
the national interest includes a strong dose of concern for the

[3] Richard P. Stebbins, ed., *Documents on American Foreign Relations, 1963*
(New York: Harper & Row, for the Council on Foreign Relations, 1964),
p. 26. The report did, in fact, make a bow toward the humanitarian motive,
as well as what one can call the enlightened self-interest motive. But these
were subordinated to the national security interest; and the national security
of the United States was seemingly, and rather blandly, equated with free-
world security—a probably valid but not self-evident proposition.

welfare of those whose existence is on the margin of subsistence. It may plausibly be argued that aid should be a feature of American policy, even were the existence of poverty in the greater part of the world unlikely to have material effects on the fortunate inhabitant of the United States. The practical politician, as well as the welfare worker, may feel that foreign assistance to the less developed is desirable even in the absence of "national security" considerations. Senator J. W. Fulbright, the Chairman of the Senate Foreign Relations Committee, has written:

> It would do us no harm to recognize that there is a moral as well as a practical and economic case for aid and that there is nothing wrong with human decency as a motive in our foreign policy. . . . We must recognize that aid is a humane as well as a practical program, that, as Woodrow Wilson said of the League of Nations, there is a "pulse of sympathy in it" and "a compulsion of conscience throughout it."[4]

If the case for aid be put in terms of the national interest, there is of course still room for including those motives of decency— even were decency not within any reasonable definition of practicality—of which Senator Fulbright spoke. The American national interest can be variously defined. Any reasonable definition will include recognition of the imponderables on which our civilization is based: the pervasive sense of responsibility, the conviction of the importance of the individual, and the belief in the possibility of man's mastery of his circumstances. It is these feelings, traditions, and beliefs which, to be practical, make a presentation to a hard-boiled congressional committee more effective if it describes the bringing of fresh water to a remote mountain village in the Andes than if it gives the cost-benefit ratio of the dam which makes that water and power possible. Both of course are necessary and relevant parts of the aid story.

[4] *New York Times Magazine,* March 21, 1965.

Both kinds of consideration are elements of any accurate appraisal of the American national interest.

The history of American aid to other countries, starting with the nineteenth-century technical missions to Central and South America, is interspersed with statements of objective and of motive, most of which evoke the mingling of the idealistic and the practical which is found in the statement by President Johnson cited at the beginning of this chapter. The Marshall Plan stressed the obligation to help our exhausted allies, but quickly became a program for rehabilitation of the defeated as well. President Truman's 1949 Inaugural Address, which made the phrase "Point Four" part of the international vocabulary, stressed the President's belief that "we should make available to peace-loving peoples the benefits of our store of technical knowledge in order to help them realize their aspirations for a better life." The 1950 legislation stated as motives both the humanitarian compulsion to struggle against hunger and the broad security interests of the United States. A decade later President Kennedy restated the point with eloquence and force, and set a precedent for a series of congressional declarations which have underscored the fortunate coincidence of what is good for others and for ourselves.

Since 1950 a variety of programs have rested on a variety of expressed (and some unexpressed) motives. Aid has been justified as a bulwark against Communist aggression or subversion. (This, too, has its humanitarian aspect, since the Communist way of life has characteristically brought neither the pleasures of freedom nor those of prosperity to the countries which have yielded to or been overcome by it.) A program like that of Public Law 480, "Food for Peace," rested both on the desire to use American food and fiber surpluses to alleviate hardship and promote development abroad and on the practical desirability of getting those surpluses out of expensive American warehouses. Motives have altered as programs have changed. Technical assistance, the heart of the Truman proposals, has a clear appeal for the humanitarian, particularly in such fields as education and health, and is thus favored by church groups and the like; while capital assistance, which has grown enormously since it was mentioned in passing in the 1949 Inaugural, has obvious attractions for the manufacturer, who tends to think of technical assistance in terms of know-how.[5]

By 1956 the United States programs were already extensive and varied. And a series of public and private studies, as yet unended, had begun, in search of a rationalizing motive. Of the studies then encouraged by both the House of Representatives and the Senate, the most widely noted was that of Max Millikan and Walt W. Rostow. They suggested "the proposition . . . that a comprehensive and sustained program of American economic assistance aimed at helping the free underdeveloped countries to create the conditions for self-sustaining economic growth can, in the short run, materially reduce the danger of conflict . . . and can, in say 2 to 3 decades, result in an overwhelming preponderance of societies with a successful record of solving their problems without resort to coercion or violence."[6]

By and large, the 1956 House and Senate hearings provided a basic and influential endorsement of long-term development as the basic purpose of aid. Action by the United States, alone and in cooperation with others, showed considerable agreement with this conclusion. In 1957 the new Development Loan Fund (DLF) began to make long-term, low-interest, development loans, repay-

[5] Obviously, these are not clear alternates. The mid-1960s brought increased recognition of the relevance of planned and substantial technical assistance not only to economic development but also to the ability to use capital assistance.

[6] Center for International Studies, M.I.T., *The Objectives of U.S. Economic Assistance Programs* (Washington: GPO, 1956), p. 20.

able in local currencies. Special efforts were then made to expand assistance to Latin America, which since World War II had received only a small part of the total of U.S. foreign aid. In 1959 the long-awaited Inter-American Development Bank was created.[7] Among other things, the Bank was given administration of a Social Progress Trust Fund, charged with making funds available for such traditionally unbankerlike purposes as public housing, land resettlement, and health.

Expansion of both institutions and programs followed. The 1960 Act of Bogotá set forth for the inter-American system the outlines of "a cooperative program of economic and social progress." In March of 1961 President Kennedy issued his call for an Alliance for Progress among the American states:

> Our Hemisphere's mission is not yet completed. For our unfulfilled task is to demonstrate to the entire world that man's unsatisfied aspiration for economic progress and social justice can be achieved by free men working within a framework of democratic institutions. . . . Therefore I have called on all the people of the Hemisphere to join in a new Alliance for Progress—Alianza para Progreso—a vast cooperative effort unparalleled in magnitude and nobility of purpose, to satisfy the basic needs of the American people for homes, work, land, health and schools. . . .[8]

The Alliance was more than funds. It established a commitment to social as well as economic progress. It marked acceptance by the leading private-enterprise economy in the world of the respectability of planning—a concept once regarded as at least

[7] Ironically enough, the Bank had long had only the lukewarm support of the United States; although pressures were growing for changes in U.S. policy toward Latin America, it was only after the Lebanese crisis brought forward the idea of an Arab Development Bank that the United States gave immediate, enthusiastic, and somewhat unexpected support to the creation of the inter-American institution.

[8] Richard P. Stebbins, ed. *Documents on American Foreign Relations, 1961* (New York: Harper & Row, for the Council on Foreign Relations, 1962), pp. 396, 397.

controversial and probably insidiously dangerous. It emphasized the necessity of cooperation between the recipients and the main financial backer, the preponderant importance of domestic resources and domestic actions, and the necessity of mobilizing additional external resources. It was, as it remains after a few alterations, a sophisticated and hopeful expression of existing wisdom in the field of economic development.

The Alliance for Progress, together with the decisions taken earlier at Bogotá, marked an enormous and quite sudden change in American official doctrine toward development in Latin America. Yet, in a sense, it was a summation of the American aid experience. In it, as in the program for other areas of the world, there appear certain constants which are basic to American aid practice. These are largely unaffected by the annual debate over aid. Definition, or identification, of such constants is obviously a highly subjective exercise. But to extract from the bewildering congeries of programs, laws, and administrations a few consistent characteristics is relevant not only to an understanding of the United States program but to the possibilities for meaningful coordination with other donors.

CONTINUITY

Friend and foe alike, in the United States, are likely to agree that aid will be with us for some years to come. It is true that opposition to large aid appropriations, or to the conduct of the program, or to both, is increasingly vocal. There is a rising tide of unease about the ability of the developing countries to absorb usefully much more than present levels of aid. The cuts made by the Congress in the appropriation requested for fiscal year 1964 were deeper than what had come to be customary. The administration's requests for appropriations in the following years have been sharply reduced, with the idea of avoiding the congressional ax. But despite voluntary or involuntary cuts the program, taking it either over all or only in its development-lending aspect, is and will undoubtedly continue to be an important part of the totality of aid available to the developing countries.

The size of the American program, and its preponderance in total world aid, underlines the importance of this element of continuity. Statistics on total aid are likely to be somewhat misleading. Proportions are affected, for example, by changes in methods of record-keeping, by altered definitions, and by better —or different—accounting. Arithmetic measurement tends to neglect, also, the problem of evaluation in determining the "aid content" of grants, soft loans, hard loans, P.L. 480 "sales," and so forth. Nevertheless, the Agency for International Development concludes that American bilateral aid disbursements in 1963 were some 49 per cent of total (bilateral *and* multilateral) aid from free-world countries. The comparable figure in 1962 was 56 per cent.[9] The same AID figures suggest that others have, in recent years, picked up a larger share of the aid "burden." Whether this suggestion is correct in the long run seems doubtful, for the U.S. share in multilateral aid has risen.[10] Even if others shoulder a larger proportion, the figures still emphasize the great importance to the developing nations of the American contribution, and consequently of the expectation that the future will bring similar amounts.

GEOGRAPHIC SCOPE

The American aid program is world-wide. It responds to needs

[9] U.S. Agency for International Development and Department of Defense, *Proposed Mutual Defense and Development Programs, FY 1966,* Summary Presentation to the Congress (Washington: March, 1965), p. 175.

[10] One expert, Jacob J. Kaplan, feels that, accurately measured, the U.S. share of aid hovered around 55 per cent of the total in the 1950s, went to 60 per cent in the 1960s, and is likely to be close to 67 per cent in the last half of this decade.

in Korea as well as India; in large countries like Brazil and in small ones like Nicaragua; in problem areas like the Congo; and in countries like Greece, Israel, or Nationalist China, where, by reason of economic progress, the more usual types of aid are being terminated. In many places AID maintains large programs and large staffs; in others it establishes merely a "presence."

The scope of the American program is such as to have aroused criticism. The Clay Committee stated its belief that "we are indeed attempting too much for too many" and mentioned without pleasure "our diffuse aid effort." Economists as well as politicians have suggested the virtue of concentrating U.S. resources; and, in fact, the bulk of American development assistance (i.e., development loans and technical assistance) now goes to a limited number of countries. Two-thirds of the $1,667 million proposed for fiscal year 1966 will go to seven countries: Brazil, Chile, Nigeria, Tunisia, India, Pakistan, and Turkey. ("Supporting assistance" funds, used to promote security or stability, are concentrated almost entirely in Korea, Jordan, Laos, and Viet-Nam.)

Nevertheless, the United States can and does make assistance available world-wide. And for many a country that aid is often large-scale if measured against the resources of the recipient, even if it is minuscule in the total aid of the donor. The consequence is American involvement wherever coordination is considered—even in Africa, where most states have strong, historic relationships with Britain, France, or Belgium.[11] Indeed, Nigeria and Tunisia are, as noted, among the largest consumers of American developmental aid.

This wide-ranging interest, and the ability to demonstrate it with assistance which can be an important part of a recipient's

[11] Angola and Mozambique are regarded by Portugal as part of its metropolitan territory.

total external resources, is an important fact in the coordinative process.

PROCUREMENT POLICY

Several shifts in U.S. aid theory have occurred over the course of the past several years. For example, grants have been de-emphasized in favor of loans. DLF loans were formerly repayable in local currency; they are now repayable, though at a remote maturity, in dollars. Development lending was at one time administered separately from other aid operations. The 1961 revision brought all aid operations together, almost swept Export-Import Bank functions into a common control with the activities of the Agency for International Development, and established AID as a semiautonomous agency within the Department of State.

One of the most significant of the changes in American aid policy was the shift from "untied" aid to that which is linked to purchases in the United States. Marshall Plan aid was subject to no special requirements of that kind, except that 50 per cent of aid-financed supplies had to move in vessels flying the American flag. In the immediate postwar period this open procurement policy had a small effect: during the greater part of the period of the Marshall Plan the United States was for practical purposes the only major supplier of the world's import needs for many industrial goods. With the postwar economic rehabilitation of Western Europe, however, open procurement with Marshall Plan dollars came to have real significance. As the economic recovery of Europe accelerated, so also did Europe's share of U.S.-financed purchases. Thus in fiscal year 1960 only 41 per cent of American aid (exclusive of the provision of surplus food and fiber under P.L. 480 and exports financed through the Export-Import Bank) was spent in the United States.

Balance of payments problems have altered this willingness to allow American official funds to finance exports from other countries. A policy of excluding the developed countries from filling orders financed by U.S. funds was adopted in the last years of the Eisenhower administration. (Procurement in Communist countries is, now as before, excluded; procurement in less developed countries, which of course are generally not substantial exporters of capital goods, is still allowed within narrow limits.) Waivers of this restriction have become increasingly difficult to obtain, as the policy of tying aid to procurement in the United States has been administered with increasing strictness. Thus in fiscal year 1963 the proportion of such procurement was 79 per cent; in 1964, 87 per cent; and an AID press release states that in February 1965 the rate was 94 per cent.

Figures of this sort are politically helpful at home. They buttress the administration's contention that balance of payments deficits do not arise from aid apropriations. They enlist important domestic support, since they emphasize the flow of orders to American companies which public aid finances. But, since they suggest that each donor may use its aid as a means of promoting exports as well as development, they obviously also underline certain problems in the coordination of aid.

EFFECTIVE USE OF AID

Increasingly, the American program has placed emphasis on self-help. The concept is, of course, not a new one. Practically every report on foreign aid has emphasized the limited and supplementary nature of external aid, the overwhelming importance of domestic savings, investment, and other policy, and the consequent dependence of the effectiveness of aid on the adequacy of the effort made by the developing nation itself.

Difficulties are inherent in the self-help doctrine. Those who need aid are likely to be those least capable of the kind of organization and administration which enacts and then enforces fair tax laws, efficiently carries through land reform, and does the other things usually thought to lie within the self-help concept. Low individual incomes, the absence of an organized capital market, and other characteristics of an underdeveloped economy may inhibit even the raising of the local currency component of development costs.

Despite problems of this sort, experience has shown that self-help can be, and indeed must be, more than a catch phrase. Many of the developing countries apply an extraordinary percentage of their gross national product to investment. Many of them have made real advances in administration, in control of inflation, and in the other measures on which advice is lavished. Substantial progress has been made in a broad span of countries, with the result that the United States has come to feel that more is not only possible but essential.

In some cases, stressing self-help as a condition of aid, which was formalized in the Act for International Development of 1961, means requiring a series of steps involving all major aspects of a country's economy: tax policies, exchange controls, governmental actions affecting private enterprise, education, and so forth. In others, a specific objective may be sought in connection with a particular aid action—for example, making disbursement of a large program loan contingent on measures to slow down the inflationary spiral, or making a loan for developing an industry dependent on the removal of impediments to the importation of raw materials for that industry.

The measurement of self-help and the determination of whether a government is, in the circumstances, doing the best that it can are difficult, especially when the actions involve the total sweep of the nation's economy. The problem of definition and of measurement of what is adequate performance by an aid recipient has thus become one of the more important issues facing the administrators of the U.S. aid program, particularly as they annually review performance with the Congress. Similarly, the setting of standards of performance in the developing countries has become a major agenda item for any effort aimed at coordinating aid policy.

PLANNING

Making self-help a major condition of aid has led beyond acceptance to the active sponsorship of planning. Prior to 1961 planning was a word hardly to be mentioned on the American political scene, least of all in connection with a congressional presentation. Even now there is some reluctance to say it outright. The variety of studies spawned after the election of President Kennedy emphasized the necessity for a coherent method of marshaling and using local and foreign resources. The Alliance for Progress, the various consortia or consultative groups, and, only to a slightly smaller extent, other aid programs involve an active American stimulation of some kind of intelligible development plans.

As AID is voluble in insisting, planning is not inconsistent with free, private enterprise. Indeed, it may be the method by which a private enterprise system may be preserved. Nevertheless, to demand that external assistance be fitted into a pattern, including a comprehensive program of ensuring that domestic savings are made and directed toward productive investment, is to state that governmental direction of resources, to an extent which only a few short years ago would have seemed inconsistent with American mores, is essential to the effective use of external aid.

How much and what kind of planning are required is another

matter. In some case, particularly in the least developed of the less developed nations (Mauritania or Chad, for example), what is needed may be not much more than a demonstration that a proposed project is economically or socially beneficial. In others, adequate planning may involve broad decisions affecting the major portion of a country's economy. What was appropriate for France under the Marshall Plan is not likely to be relevant to the present needs of Tanzania. The kind of plan produced by Pakistan is not likely to fit the circumstances of Upper Volta. What is desired is that degree of planning which is really a facet of self-help—a demonstrable effort to use aid intelligently, along with other domestic and external resources.

Consistent with its concern for the optimum use of resources is the U.S. endorsement of "program" loans. Although the edges of the distinctions blur, program loans generally support the development of an economy, while project loans finance specific facilities. Typically, program loans finance the purchase of raw materials, replacement parts, or other items necessary to maintain or increase production from existing plant. Project loans, on the other hand, tend to finance new construction. They are generally preferred by some institutions, like the World Bank, and by some donor governments, like Germany.

For the lender, the advantages of project lending stem in part from his ability to inspect the facility built with his money. It gives him greater possibilities of supervising the use of his funds and ensuring their application to a developmental purpose. If a loan finances construction of a factory, the lender can usually ensure that it will be built according to acceptable standards, that its construction will be adequately supervised, and that provision for its operation after completion will be made. Hopefully, he will later be able to point with pride to its sound conception and construction, to its contribution to reducing foreign-exchange expenditures or to expanding imports. He can also arrange to have a plaque affixed to the building making clear the origin of the funds which financed it, so that he obtains political kudos—or guarantees that it will be the first target of a riot of local nationalists. Program loans, on the other hand, diffuse their benefits more widely throughout the economy. Their effects are less immediately visible; their proper use is often more difficult to ensure. These are the kinds of loans on which the Marshall Plan was based; but there are experts who suggest that many of the developing countries may have neither the administrative structure nor the sense of responsibility necessary to make sure that program loans are not used unwisely at best or for the benefit of something other than development at worst.

The United States uses program loans more extensively than most other donors.[12] There is some reason to suspect that American practice has favored program lending at least in some cases because it provided a quick but respectable way of pumping funds into a faltering economy. In some other cases, as where a loan is made for a "program" consisting of a series of projects later to be individually approved, it has been chiefly a label used for administrative purposes. But, in general, the nature of the American aid program is such as to favor a lending technique that emphasizes the total needs of a developing economy. For many recipients, the size of the American program and the degree of responsibility assumed by the United States orient thinking on both sides toward over-all development and use of all the resources of the country, including existing plant, and toward reduced emphasis on the construction of a new facility. Obviously, objectives overlap, just as techniques are often

[12] But note that France and the United Kingdom also emphasize program aid or alternative "general purposes" devices. See below, pp. 45 and 49.

hard to distinguish: if a sound factory is built with German funds, it will contribute to the economy; if raw materials or equipment are financed by the United States which keep other factories functioning, they or their employees will consume the output of the German-financed factory.

MULTILATERALIZATION [13]

Finally, placing the imprimatur of some kind of international approval on American lending has become at least symbolically important.

There is substantial sentiment in the United States for multilateral, rather than bilateral, development lending. The Clay Committee—one of its strongest members being, notably, a former president of the World Bank—strongly recommended multilateral over bilateral aid. On the ground that multilateral aid is more objective, less subject to political pressures, and better able to obtain reforms without incurring the ire of the recipient, Senator Fulbright has strongly endorsed turning over development lending to the World Bank or similar institutions. The 1965 version of the legislation authorizing foreign aid made 15 per cent of development lending funds available to the World Bank. However, the authority to use the World Bank in lending AID development funds was negated by various conditions placed in the appropriations act. It would be unfortunate if this precedent were to establish a pattern.

There is additional reason for the United States to encourage contributions to such agencies as the soft-loan affiliate of the World Bank, the International Development Association; in IDA forty cents of each American dollar is matched by sixty cents

---

[13] This is one of those words which are both so clumsy and general in meaning as to be objectionable to linguists and logicians alike. It has nevertheless the useful capacity of suggesting, without defining, cooperation among a number of states, the sense in which it is used here.

contributed by others. (But less than 40 per cent of IDA procurement is made in the United States.) Moreover, smaller donors of aid funds may well find it desirable, for reasons which include both the wish not to be caught in the competitive struggle among applicants for funds and an awareness of the high administrative costs of giving away relatively small amounts of money, to funnel their contributions to development through international agencies. Some, like Canada, which has made some $50 million available to Latin America (restricting procurement to Canada) via the Inter-American Development Bank, find the channel of an internationl agency highly useful.

Nevertheless, aid remains preponderantly bilateral and seems likely, for the major aid donors, to continue so. The primary reason, already mentioned, is that aid is a substantial element in the political relations of the donor states with the less developed countries. To take the politics out of aid is likely to put an end to the aid.

Where aid is in the form of "supporting assistance"—for example, the bulk of American economic aid to Viet-Nam—national political interests are so closely involved that coordination is unlikely except with other donors having very similar political commitments. But even where aid is clearly developmental in purpose, each of the major donors is more than likely to retain control of its funds and resolutely to keep its aid chiefly bilateral. This being so (and in no major donor nation other than the United States has there been much pressure for multilateralization of development grants or loans), the need for devices which can effectively coordinate these various programs is all the more underlined.

*　　　*　　　*

In sum: The United States program rests upon censensus that aid must serve the national interest, though there hardly seems to be consensus as to what that national interest is. It is a large program, important to the prospective or actual recipients of major funds, because it can have a very appreciable effect on their economies. It responds to world-wide needs, though there is increasing tendency to concentrate the major share of the funds in a limited number of countries. Given the totals, however, what remains is important even to the countries not so favored. Aid is tied to procurement in the United States. Self-help and performance are increasingly emphasized, with the concomitant of insistence on adequate planning and on the tools that make planning effective. There is a mounting desire and pressure for multilateralization of aid, but the reasons and the proposals vary among its advocates and their success has been limited.

Programs Stemming from Colonial Association

Any classification of aid donors is bound to be arbitrary. Programs might, for example, be grouped by the geographic area in which they operate, by their emphasis on technical or on capital assistance, or by their methodology. For an inquiry focused largely upon coordination of bilateral aid, the criterion which seems most relevant is that of the kind of national interest which lies behind each donor's aid program. From this point of view, the otherwise dissimilar programs of France, the United Kingdom, Belgium, the Netherlands, and Portugal (and the bilateral program of the multilateral European Economic Community) can be considered together. Each is based on a history of close political, economic, and cultural ties with existing or former colonial territories and would surely not exist in its present form where it not for these long-standing relationships. The wide differences in the size of these programs, in their geographic spread, in their terms, and in the way in which they are run are leveled by a common denominator of motive.[14] Each of these donor countries has made the decision that the national interest is served by assistance to states or overseas governmental units with which there have been historic political ties. Each, for the major part and with some exceptions, largely limits aid to recipients in that category. This is almost as true for Britain, with its widespread assistance to countries circling the globe, as for Belgium.

These programs, accordingly, show a natural propensity to concentrate aid in certain areas. The nature of the over-all relationship also influences the kind of aid given. Aid, particularly that of France, is largely provided on a grant basis, is often used to finance general governmental expenses, generally provides assistance on a nonproject basis, and includes a high proportion of technical assistance in the total program. Finally, some of these donors regard as aid certain items, both in technical and in capital assistance programs, which stem from the colonial past and which are dubiously included in even a broad definition of aid —items such as financing of external debt owed largely to the mother country, or provision for the salaries or retirement compensation of its nationals.

[14] It is emphatically not suggested that these motives, or reasons for aid, particularly when used as a basis for classifying donors, are exact, or rigid, or exclusive. Italy, which is otherwise classified for present purposes, has a former colonial association with Somalia and other African states. Whatever the U.S. relation to Latin America may be, it is surely something special. The categories here are suggestive—intended more to promote realistic discussion of coordinative problems and prospects than to establish a new set of (perhaps questionable) concepts.

FRANCE

The largest aid program after the American is that of France. Emulating the already noted American tendency toward re-examination of the theory and practices of aid, the French in 1963 subjected their policies and programs to analysis. The examination was conducted by a specially constituted Commission of Inquiry, headed by a former minister, Professor Jean-Marcel Jeanneney. Somewhat surprisingly, and perhaps disingenuously, the commission rejected economic advantage as a valid reason for aid: it postulated the simple duty to aid those whose circumstances required help. Second, it stressed France's need or duty to diffuse its civilization; it asserted the universal validity of that civilization and, consequently, the legitimate desire of the French nation peaceably to implant it in foreign parts. The general diplomatic and other advantages of an aid program were regarded as of some importance, though hard to define. But the Jeanneney Commission argued that, despite the Western interest, shared by France, in preventing the formation of a large bloc of hostile developing nations, aid should not become an instrument of the East-West struggle. The French tradition of revolution with freedom and the fact that France considered itself not to be one of the major contending powers in the cold war were considered likely to gain receptiveness for a French presence and for French ideas both in the developing and in the developed countries.

The French program, which runs close to a billion dollars annually,[15] is heavily concentrated. In 1963 94 per cent of bilateral aid went to Franc Area countries. Of the 6 per cent going

[15] Detailed aid figures for the DAC members are given in the Appendix Table. The figures in the text are taken from OECD or DAC reports, but they are in no way a complete statistical analysis of any country's aid pro-

outside that area, a substantial part went to countries which were formerly parts of French Indo-China. Of some $690 million in bilateral grants, only $25 million went outside the Franc Area, of which over $8 million went to the successor states of Indo-China.

When the present beneficiaries of French aid were administered from Paris, the central authority collected revenues and distributed proceeds in the form of schools and hospitals, and salaries of technicians and officials. A close and similar relationship continues to exist between France and its aid recipients, despite independence and the cutting off of the direct flow of tax revenues to the French treasury. It is for this reason that a large proportion of French aid is in the form of grants, both for capital expenditures and for technical assistance. Also, the French continue, for this reason or out of habit acquired during the colonial period,[16] to provide funds for budgetary support—a form of aid which is regarded in the United States with suspicion and is thought to be justifiable, under current doctrine, only in such extreme cases as Jordan or Bolivia. Even a good deal of what the French classify as technical assistance could as well be called budget sup-

gram. As they necessarily apply to single years, too much weight should not be attached to them. Nevertheless, they do suggest the outlines of the kind of program each donor mounts, generally year after year.

[16] A great deal of what is done in aid seems to be based either on habit or on current fashions in nomenclature. Whether results are less desirable than would otherwise be the case is doubtful; the theories of aid practice change frequently. Sometimes, but not always, so does the practice itself; sometimes the change is only verbal. Since 1961 U.S. policy, for example, has favored long-term loans, rather than grants; but a forty-year no-interest loan, with a ten-year grace period, is the substantial equivalent of a loan on commercial terms of one-half of the amount involved, and a grant of the other half. Until 1964 the Canadians insisted that soft, long-term loans were, in fact, an anomaly, and either should be on terms which would pay the lender the cost of borrowing or should be given outright as grants; since then, they have added soft loans to their aid program. The United States has sometimes thought grants were more appropriate than loans, sometimes the

port, since it finances governmental functions. Thus, of the 45,000 French citizens serving overseas in technical assistance capacities, 43,500 serve in Africa in former French possessions; and a substantial proportion of them perform governmental or semigovernmental duties.

Since 1963 there has been some reorientation of the French aid program. It has slightly extended its geographic and political limits. France is now a member of the Indian and Pakistani consortia, as well as, though more nominally, of the OECD consortia for Greece and Turkey. A substantial credit to Mexico has been arranged; and both the suggestions of the Jeanneney report and the 1964-65 statements of General de Gaulle indicate that more attention will be paid to Latin America, perhaps also to other areas where special political circumstances so warrant.

A supplementary report filed by former Ambassador Jean Chauvel, one of the members of the Jeanneney Commission, argues that French aid, being an important instrument of diplomatic influence, should not be spread too thin, nor should it be attempted where it could play no significant role. Hence, countries like India and Pakistan, which are considered important by other major donors, would appear to have a low priority. The explicitly political justification of aid in the Chauvel memorandum would forecast an increase of the French effort in the Middle East, on the basis of ties of culture and language, and in Latin America, where the local desire for less dependence on

---

opposite. The explanation for the French use of grants would seem thus to be more the fact that this is the way it was done before, and the unpleasant political consequences of changing from an easier to a harder form of aid, than the fact that the recipient receives more economic benefit in the long run from a grant than from a loan.

It may be noted, however, that, perhaps as a result of comparisons induced by DAC, France is reducing its contributions to outright budgetary support, and that the proportion of loans in over-all French aid is rising.

the United States is thought to provide an opening for French influence. Ambassador Chauvel also suggested that where special circumstances like these do not obtain, the French aid effort should be guided largely by commercial criteria; that is, its contribution to expansion of French exports—a conclusion somewhat different from that of his colleagues.

In summary: The French program is sizable in absolute terms and large in terms of ratio to gross national product. It emphasizes grants rather than loans, and is based on past, or possibly anticipated, French cultural and political ties with recipients. These ties influence both the scope of the program, by limiting it largely to Africa or Southeast Asia, and its nature, by directing it toward technical assistance (principally teachers and administrators) and toward capital assistance for governmental functions and infrastructure. Where the French give aid and these cultural and political links are weak or lacking, as in Turkey or India or Mexico, terms are hard and are based mainly on an export credit rationale. The political interest in such aid may be roughly measured by the extent to which the commercial terms of export credits are sweetened by linked government-to-government long-term loans.[17] Some expansion of a soft-loan policy may be expected if political advantage can be seen in it.

THE UNITED KINGDOM

The British White Paper on Aid to Developing Countries presented to Parliament in September 1963 was rather shorter on philosophy and longer on facts than the Jeanneney report. It

[17] Since 1963 the French have used an aid "cocktail." For example, the large credit granted in 1964 to Mexico consisted of a substantial medium-term export credit and a soft government-to-government loan, the proceeds of which could be used for purposes associated with utilization of the export credit.

remarked upon the increasing gap between the standards of living in the developed and less developed nations, recalled that aid might legitimately be regarded as a means of promoting "stability in the developing countries," and suggested that their economic progress, with stability, should prove to be to the benefit of the donors as well as of the recipients. Beyond these points of guidance, the White Paper contained no recommendations. It did recount the British position on a number of matters, including tied aid, and it did point out the recent measures which Britain had decided to take to make aid available on easier terms to recipients needing such assistance. This theme was re-emphasized in a White Paper presented to Parliament on August 3, 1965.

The French and British reports are as dissimilar in tone as popular caricatures of the two nations might suggest. And the British are either too restrained or too uncertain at present of its validity to stress the "civilizing mission" rationale for their activities abroad which seems to inspire Gaullist pronouncements. But the two governments are alike in recognizing the historic basis of their aid programs, and in emphasizing that their aid is and should be channeled to countries with which their political ties have been long and close.

British aid has been running somewhat over $400 million annually. Like that of France, it is heavily concentrated in countries with traditional political ties. Because of the nature of the Commonwealth, however, it is much more widely distributed to a vastly larger number of people than is French aid. There has been a tendency toward further expansion in recent years. In 1961 dependent and independent territories of the Commonwealth received 93 per cent of official United Kingdom bilateral loans and grants. By 1963 the percentage had decreased to 86 per cent, of which roughly half went to colonies. Disbursements to non-Commonwealth countries have grown threefold in the period 1959-65, and the proportion is expected to increase further.

The largest part of British aid is disbursed as loans to independent countries under the British Export Guarantees Act, with the former colonies receiving the largest amounts. Terms have been typically for a loan period of twenty-five years, with a grace period on capital repayment of seven years, and a 6 per cent interest rate, the rate being based on the cost of money in the London capital market. In 1964 the British, however, announced their intention of granting grace periods on interest in suitable situations—that is, where there is demonstrable need for soft terms, and where other donors are also prepared to soften their terms; and, as confirmed at the July 1965 DAC high-level meeting, some British loans will now be on terms like those of the International Development Association.

Like the French, the British make substantial grants, as well as loans, for administration in dependent territories and for such services as education, health, and water supply. British capital aid is largely of the program type, directed toward general development needs of the economy more than to specific projects.

British aid is tied to British exports. In 1963-64 London experimented with a device which was hoped to be useful both at home and abroad, by allocating additional funds for purchases by less developed countries from industries in Britain which are operating at substantially less than capacity. It was thought that this would make additional aid available, and not merely shift the incidence of what would otherwise be aid-financed export orders. Though the program was somewhat tentatively compared to the American food-for-peace program—Britain exporting surplus industrial capacity rather than surplus food and fiber—it seems to have been abandoned for lack of success.

OTHER PROGRAMS

As might be expected, Belgium's aid goes almost wholly to former colonies in Africa; in 1963 three-quarters of it went to the former Belgian Congo, the remainder to Rwanda and Burundi. Belgium has made a modest effort toward a wider geographic coverage in its aid. It is a member of the consortia for India, Pakistan, Turkey, and Greece. Turkey received a loan of $1.3 million, on terms of 3 per cent and a maturity of twenty years. Assistance to India and Pakistan was by way of medium-term export guarantees.

Netherlands aid has been, like Belgium's, substantial, but it took a sharp drop in 1963 when the program for West New Guinea came to an end along with Dutch rule over that territory. It remains to be seen whether the reduction in total aid will be permanent. That probably depends largely on future relations with Indonesia, a country which, after independence, seemed determined to get its "Western aid" by the more direct method of seizing Dutch (and other) property.

Portugal states as the basic aim of its aid policy the promotion of the harmonious development of mainland and overseas Portuguese territories. It is thus hardly surprising that Portuguese aid, except for small contributions to multilateral agencies, goes entirely to Portuguese overseas territories, mainly to Angola and Mozambique. The Portuguese made 17 per cent of their aid available as grants in 1963, while the 83 per cent which is loans was at interest rates of 2.5 per cent and for periods of twenty years. That has been the continuing pattern.

Programs with No Colonial Association

Other DAC countries—the German Federal Republic, Italy, and Japan—owe a common characteristic partially to their having been the losers in one or both world wars. None has the benefits or the burdens of recent extensive overseas possessions or dependencies. Such direct responsibilities as they might have felt have been sloughed off by the events either of 1914-18 or of 1939-45. The beneficiaries of their aid are not recent political dependencies in the sense of, say, the relationship of the Congo to Belgium. Italy and Japan feel substantial ties to nearby developing countries—Italy in the Mediterranean area, Japan in Southeast Asia. But these are ties to independent countries. And, apart from the Italian program in Somalia, a former colony, neither Italy nor Japan shows the kind of preponderant concentration of capital, technicians, trade, and investment that characterizes a relationship like that, for example, of France with Gabon.

All three have experienced a strong economic revival since the ebb years of 1948 or 1949. Germany and Japan have carried substantial reparations charges which, somewhat dubiously, are reported to DAC as development assistance. (Italy also has paid some reparations.) All have programs of considerable size, with Germany's by far the largest, as well as the most widespread geographically, and Italy's the smallest. German net aid flow, bilateral and by way of contributions to international organizations, came to some $460 million in 1964, compared to $178 million for Japan and $56 million for Italy. Commitment figures for the same year illustrate the difficulty of relying on any one year's statistics to prove a trend. Total official bilateral commitments for 1964 were: Germany—$467 million; Japan—$259 million; and Italy—$111 million.

German aid has tended to follow and support German trade. This has meant a rather wide geographic distribution, with Africa, the Near East, South Asia, and Latin America all being substantial recipients; it has also meant rather short-term, export-financing types of lending. German loans have, however, since 1961 become more developmental in nature, with interest rates going down and maturities lengthening.[18]

The Japanese program has largely been one of relatively short-term export credits, with relatively high interest rates, tied to the cost of money in Japan. The credits have gone to countries in the Far East, to Latin America, and one recently to Africa. Italians loans have carried high interest rates, but some have been freer than others in financial terms—that is, as a rule they have not been tied to purchases in Italy, though the effects of this untying are not great.

Canada, with neither the taint nor the advantages of a colonial past, exercises relative geographic and political freedom in the choice of aid recipients. It does, however, recognize political associations, by placing the bulk of its program in the Commonwealth; hemispheric geography, by taking a lively interest in Latin America; and political-linguistic realities at home, by showing a somewhat special interest in French-speaking Africa. On the one side, Canada thus stresses the consultative arrangements of the Colombo Plan; on the other, the major expansion of its aid program has been in Latin America. Until 1963-64, Canada maintained that aid should be in grant form, with export guarantees financing trade where necessary. In 1964 a program of long-term soft loans, comparable to those extended by the International Development Association, was initiated.

Other DAC members—Denmark, Norway, Austria, and Sweden —have smaller aid programs suited to their own resources and political inclinations. The Norwegian and Danish programs are small, though in some cases important, particularly in the field of technical assistance and in the provision of capital associated with that assistance. Austria's program is largely confined to contributions to multilateral agencies, although it is a

18 For a discussion of "terms of aid" see pps. IV-36 ff.

member of the consortium for Turkey, and has there made a $0.9 million loan. It has also made a $1.8 million loan to India, and has facilitated sales of IBRD securities in Austria.

Sweden, a member so recent that it did not participate in the 1965 aid review, and Switzerland, not yet a member, have programs like those of Austria and Norway. Aid from these countries is relatively small, both in absolute amount (Sweden is the leader) and in relation to gross national product.[19] Sweden has favored using the facilities of the World Bank. Since the assistance of these countries carries few political overtones, their aid may be particularly useful in those situations in which a recipient seeks to avoid involvement in the East-West struggle, while not sacrificing needed assistance.

The Swiss program is not likely to present problems of coordination very different from those of the nations with which it is associated in the OECD. Special arrangements can always be worked out for those cases in which there is a special interest. A certain nervous hesitancy—perhaps financial in nature—seems to keep Switzerland out of the DAC. The recent accession of Austria and Sweden may possibly induce the Swiss to take the not very icy plunge.

The European Economic Community

Aside from the bilateral programs, the five DAC members which also belong to the European Economic Community (France, the German Federal Republic, Italy, the Netherlands,

[19] Additionally, particularly in Switzerland, substantial assistance is given by private organizations—church groups, clubs, and the like. (The same is notably true of the United States and of church groups, in particular, in Germany. The outflow of private help reaches amounts difficult to estimate, but certainly large.) These private good works are largely in the field of technical assistance, and resemble in some measure the activities of the great American foundations.

Belgium; Luxembourg is not a DAC member) have their own multilateral program which provides funds via three instrumentalities: the European Development Fund (EDF), the general budget of the Community, and the European Investment Bank. Commitments for these three sources in 1963 were $84 million, of which the bulk was from the EDF and the European Investment Bank. Under the Second Convention of Association, which came into effect on June 1, 1964, for a five-year period, these two institutions should have $800 million at their disposal, compared with $581 million for the previous five-year period.

Like the former colonial powers, the EEC makes aid available to former overseas territories of EEC members. The period 1958-63 showed EDF funds going 88 per cent to the Franc Area, 5 per cent to former Belgian territories, 6 per cent to former Dutch territories, and 1 per cent to former Italian territories. Under the 1964 Convention, EDF funds are to go to the states associated with the EEC ($730 million) and the dependent countries and territories ($70 million). Additional amounts, largely as technical assistance and as social and economic investment, will go to the African states associated economically with France.

The Community uses grants more than loans, which have been kept to the relatively small average amount of $1.6 million. In the next period, it is anticipated that $50 million of EDF "special loans" will be made, in productive operations of general value to the recipient. Technical assistance and construction of roads, harbor improvement, and other elements of "infrastructure" will continue to be financed by grants.

The European Investment Bank, on the other hand, uses loans for its program designed to facilitate the entry of Greece and Turkey into the Common Market, but at rates of interest which may be subsidized from the EDF grant fund.

The Rationale for Coordination

These, then, are the outlines of the programs of aid of the developed countries of the free world.[20] The programs are often similar. Many objectives are shared. But the programs also exhibit differences in techniques, size and scope, and purposes.

Broadly speaking, at home and abroad each donor justifies its program of aid by the needs of the countries it is helping. Each has a program designed to contribute to economic and social progress in those countries. Each emphasizes in its public statements the conviction that humanitarian motives would, in the absence of any other rationale, be a sufficient reason for the continuation of aid.

Beyond this, all consider that efforts to speed the growth of the less developed countries are in the interest of the developed nations. They share a concern with the lagging pace of development, and they worry about the political instability which is the likely concomitant of an unsatisfactory rate of improvement in economies in which enormous numbers of people exist at a bare subsistence level. They are concerned with the disparities in living standards within the developing nations. They seek aid policies which will contribute not only to growth but equally to a substantial betterment of the lot of the least privileged citizens of the developing nations.

[20] It must be noted that each of the outlines is designed only to make comparative analysis possible, not to furnish a complete description. It should also be emphasized that there are, of course, substantial aid programs, operating largely with "Western" funds, which are not described here because they are not within the purview of the DAC. Australia, Israel, and others are donors. There are also, importantly, the programs of the multilateral agencies: the UN, via the Special Fund; the IBRD, IFC, and IDA; the regional institutions, such as the Inter-American Development Bank; as well as the considerable contributions, mostly in technical assistance, by the large family of UN specialized agencies such as FAO and UNESCO. Nor, as noted above, should the considerable amount of private aid be overlooked.

With these interests and purposes in common, there exist important differences between the DAC members, differences which in some cases approach the seriousness of conflicts. The humanitarian base for each program is generously laced with considerations, broad or narrow, of national interest. These may be political, economic, or commercial. The stated desire of France to exploit its cultural association with Latin America and to increase its political influence there may well cause French aid in Central and South America to be viewed in Washington with more suspicion than gratification. American aid to Tunisia is said to have been one of the causes of some French disaffection with that country. While the United States was competing with the Soviet Union in assistance to Indonesia, the Dutch may not have thought the American program entirely helpful to their efforts to reach settlement of economic issues outstanding between them and Sukarno.

On the economic and commercial side, competition is even more evident. Each aid program recognizes the trade and export benefits which aid may bring, as well as the more generalized economic benefits of these trade relations. Some of the programs rest very heavily indeed on their financing of exports from the donor nation. All derive substantial domestic support from the fact of such exports. Even where purposes agree, there are significant differences in doctrine and practice. And, though all are committed to an improved flow of resources from the rich to the poor, within that commitment a world of significant conflict can be—and sometimes is—accommodated.

In these circumstances one might well question the validity of a "common" aid effort and of that mutuality of purposes which is the *sine qua non* of the DAC.

On the other hand, it is these very differences, plus the necessary condition of an objective to which all subscribe, that give opportunity and importance to a coordinative mechanism. Complete agreement would probably make an apparatus of coordination redundant; complete disagreement—or disagreement so fundamental as that which, for example, exists between the United States and Communist China—would make it economically ineffective and politically impossible. Among the DAC members, as a glance at their programs shows, there is both agreement and conflict. The broad purposes of the common aid effort are adhered to by the DAC members (as well as by like-minded states outside the organization). At the same time, their programs reveal not only administrative or doctrinal differences, but conflicting commercial or political ends. The situation is thus, in a sense, ideal for a coordinative effort: the opportunity to increase the area of agreement and decrease that of disagreement or of conflict is evident.

Whether there is need for such an effort is a separate question, although one is tempted to regard the answer as self-evident. The establishment of the DAC postulated rather than demonstrated both the opportunity and the need. Nor did that establishment define, except in the broadest sense, the desired coordination. Nevertheless, that the DAC was set up suggests a general conviction on the part of those with considerable experience and large interest in the matter that the broadly agreed goal —improvement of the lot of the poor of the world—was more likely to be attained if donors were in reasonable concert than if they were not. It is important that the DAC exists not to conduct a dispassionate inquiry into its basic postulate but to prove it. In its works more than its words one is likely to find both definition and demonstration of the substantive content of that mutuality which is assumed in "the common aid effort."

It might seem logical to expand this effort toward mutuality beyond the DAC. There are donors other than the DAC members: certain other Western or neutralist states with small programs; the United Nations and its family of regional economic organizations and specialized agencies (including, more or less formally, the IBRD group); and the Communist countries. Presumably, a developing country would profit from rationalization of all outside assistance, whatever its source.

However logical such a conclusion might seem, its extensive realization is not likely. Coordination by DAC members with the World Bank family of institutions is relatively easy. Tradition, membership, and weighted voting there ensure a substantial identity of interest with the DAC membership, although within that over-all understanding there is ample room for disagreement. Coordination *with* the United Nations—the Special Fund, or a universal but specialized agency like UNESCO—by ensuring, for example, that an AID program in the field of health complements and does not overlap a World Health Organization program, is more difficult, but still within the realm of the possible. Coordination *through* the United Nations—that is, allowing a UN representative or UN body to allocate resources—seems, on the other hand, very remote.

This is not to say that the Development Assistance Committee is the only, or the best, method for coordination. In many cases it is not the appropriate mechanism, even among its limited membership of "like-minded" states. Where it has been agreed that joint action, to the extent permitted by the continuing bilateral nature of most aid, will be undertaken for a recipient, the consortium is better suited to the kind of operative decisions which have to be taken. Where a general political association is the essence of the cooperative effort, the impeccable objectives and conference techniques of the Colombo Plan are appropriate. When development assistance comes largely from a single donor with particularly close political associations with recipients, the technique may be that of the Alliance for Progress, or may be consultative sessions like those organized by the French with the associated states of Africa.

Whatever the nature and extent of the technique which is used, however, none vests any great responsibility in a UN body or in the UN representative who is present in most developing nations —even in the area of technical assistance to which UN aid is limited. The missions of the bilateral donors in those countries generally maintain toward him a correct but distant relationship. For this attitude, there are several reasons: bilateral aid is a part of national foreign policy; and the United Nations as a whole is not always "like-minded" with the donor. The United States, for example, would likely not regard as especially desirable the coordinative efforts of a Soviet citizen (however internationalized by his oath of loyalty to the United Nations) who might be the UN representative in La Paz or Dar-es-Salaam.[21]

The problem arises out of the fact that there are some 115 members of the United Nations, the majority of whom have views on many matters, including aid policy, very different from those of the little band of DAC members. Among those 115 are some seventy-seven members of a rather formally constituted bloc of less developed nations;[22] and there are the Communist states, plus those which generally vote with them. The lines, of course, cut in various directions: Latin America is in the group of seventy-seven, but also in the Alliance for Progress. But none of the developed non-Communist nations is likely to wish for the type

[21] The point is, however, rather theoretical, at least until now. The U.S.S.R. has furnished to the United Nations very few persons for such appointments.

[22] Assembled at the 1964 United Nations Conference on Trade and Development.

of "coordination" which might emerge from the United Nations.

If social and economic development are the goal, however, some means of cooperation between the various programs should be attainable. Such UN agencies as the Special Fund do carry on programs coordinated in fact with those of bilateral donors. So also do the FAO, UNESCO, and others. Within the limits set by the national interest aspects of bilateral aid and the policy differences which separate UN members, it is possible that the Trade and Development Board of the United Nations, when it begins substantive work, may make some progress. But, given the East-West differences in long-term objectives, the prospects do not seem bright. Between the DAC members the degree of difference is wide enough to make coordination desirable, and narrow enough to make it possible. For the present, the conflicting differences in purpose between the Communist and the Western nations are so wide as to make broad coordination not really possible and, in many cases, probably not desirable. It may well be, however, that on certain specific projects the purposes of East and West may be close enough to make possible some measure of coordination and cooperation, just as both sides see reason in contributing to such agencies as the Special Fund of the United Nations.

Impetus may, however, come from the side of the recipients. For them, at least, the uncomplicated objective is development and growth, though presumably in the context of their individual political and social philosophies. That purpose may require the recipient to organize the flow of capital and of technical assistance in such a way as to extract from it the maximum in progress. To do this, in turn, requires some kind of coordinating apparatus at the receiving end, if it does not exist at the giving end. The result may be greater future emphasis by the developing nations on the facilities of the United Nations, and particularly on the assistance which it can give to recipients in organizing their own administrative structures.

In these circumstances coordination has more than slight importance. Whether it is attained or not, or to what degree, will be a reasonable measure of the mutuality of high purpose which ought to underlie not merely a mechanism like the DAC but the entirety of the free world's aid programs.

Chapter III

The Development
Assistance Committee:
Doctrine and Procedure

To divide the world as between the aiding and the
aided is both wrong and psychologically damaging.
J. K. GALBRAITH, *Economic Development*

The Development Assistance Committee owes its existence to
the confluence of several forces. One of these is the tendency of
the times to create a coordinating committee in any situation in
which several entities have similar but not identical programs
or policies. Conceivably this tendency, an extension to the international field of an instinct already long evident domestically,
might have been sufficient in itself to bring about an organization like the DAC, at least as soon as the several programs of
aid became important enough so that divergencies were both
noticeable and irksome.

Additionally, the 1960s saw the development of aid as a regular
and continuing aspect of the foreign relations of a number of
states. Where aid to the less developed had once been a matter
of the intermittent act of charity or a program of reconstruction
—relieving the suffering of the victims of earthquake or flood
or war—it had become by 1960 a major enterprise not only for

the United States but also for several of the nations which had achieved reconstruction and revitalization of their economies. In such circumstances it seemed but rational that the donors, states previously associated in the reconstruction effort, should discuss attaining the mutual aims of their efforts to assist the developing nations of the world. And experience, limited though it was, reinforced the conclusion that problems as well as opportunities existed in sufficient numbers to make a coordinative mechanism, of some sort, useful.

At the same time, the growing prosperity of the postwar Western world made it evident that the prime task of the Organization for European Economic Cooperation, as the main instrument of the Marshall Plan and the chief vehicle for supervising the administration of American reconstruction aid to a war-torn Europe, had been accomplished. But it seemed to many that the OEEC should not be buried in the moment of its success. It had, under the Marshall Plan, opened the vistas of an effective and mutually beneficial economic cooperation between like-minded states. The problems of the 1960s were likely to be different, but no less difficult or important, than those of the immediate postwar period. The resurgent nations and their erstwhile benefactor might well find benefit in a voluntary and cooperative effort. Adding these weighty considerations to the observable precept that an international organization is seldom destroyed if it can be reorganized, the Organization for Economic Cooperation and Development rose, in October 1961, from the warm ashes of the OEEC.

For some time before, the problems of the several programs of bilateral aid had been under discussion. As European prosperity brought Marshall Plan assistance to an end, it also gave rise to the American thought that those who had been helped might well take a more vigorous role than they seemed to be doing in assisting the less developed nations. With this thought probably in mind, the Under Secretary of State at the time, Douglas Dillon, made a statement at a meeting in Paris in January 1960 which was considering the fate of the OEEC. Mr. Dillon's suggestion, insofar as here relevant, was to the effect that attention should be given to two important tasks: (a) enlarging the flow of development capital from the industrialized to the less developed areas of the world; and (b) finding a mechanism for continuing Western cooperation on major economic problems, including those of development assistance.

Reorganization of the OEEC was proposed. Pending that reorganization, a limited group was to be constituted to consider the substantive problems of development assistance and the better coordination of the bilateral aid programs. This group, the United States felt, should operate on an informal basis, should consult as desirable with other international organizations, and should include "those countries in a position to make an effective long-term bilateral contribution to the flow of funds to the less-developed countries."

The Development Assistance Group (DAG) was thus established at the 1960 Paris meeting. After the formation of the OECD, in October 1961, the "Group" was transmuted into the "Committee"—a part of the OECD but with a number of structural evidences of its independent past, some of which have a certain importance.

The Development Assistance Group was peripatetic. Its meetings were held in Washington, Bonn, Tokyo, and London. When it became the Development Assistance Committee, it settled into its present quarters, as part of the OECD, at the Château de la Muette.

Doctrine

The DAC starts with the assumption that bilateral aid programs may usefully be considered by a group limited to the free-world donors of aid. It continues with what is implicit in the formation of any coordinating group: that consultation is in the interest of the members of the group. What may be called its doctrine, resting on these premises, is that such a group can be helpful to, and is responsible to, the recipients as well as the donors of aid. From the outset, therefore, the DAC has made its task not merely coordination, but also improvement of the aid efforts of its membership.

Improvement has generally meant mainly (a) increasing the flow of assistance, capital and technical, to the less developed countries; and (b) doing so in terms less onerous to the recipient than those currently prevailing. Latterly, more sophisticated concepts have gained fashion. Since the effectiveness of aid is considered to depend on a multiplicity of factors, such as self-help and the "mix" of technical and capital assistance, it is sometimes argued that making the aid package larger and softer does not necessarily result in "improved" aid—that the problems of development are such as to require a diagnosis which is more sophisticated and more individual than the simple, universal prescription of more aid at easier terms.

The DAC early formulated its agreed doctrine concerning the volume of aid. A Resolution on the Common Aid Effort, adopted at the DAG meeting of March 1961, declared the group to be conscious of the aspirations of the less developed countries to achieve improved living standards for their peoples. It stated that the group was convinced of the need for assistance, and agreed to recommend to members "that they should make it their common objective to secure an expansion of the aggregate volume of resources made available to the less developed countries and to improve their effectiveness."

This resolution is one of the main threads of DAC doctrine. It is buttressed by the resolution adopted at the 1964 United Nations Conference on Trade and Development, which provided: "Each economically advanced country should endeavor to supply . . . financial resources to the less developed countries of a minimum net amount approaching as nearly as possible to 1 per cent of its national income, having regard, however, to the special position of certain countries which are net importers of capital."[1] All DAC members approved the resolution; and, in their annual meeting of July 1965, they reiterated their commitment to this target.

The other main body of doctrine concerns "terms of aid"— the question of grants as against loans, of hard as against soft lending, of the proper "mix" of an aid program. The task forces set up after the election of President Kennedy concluded that easier terms of aid were a necessity if the less developed countries, or at least some of them, were to be able to meet the increasing burden of servicing their foreign debt, including that from "developmental" loans which in many cases carried relatively short maturities and high rates of interest. The 1961 review of aid doctrine in the United States therefore led to an American policy of forty-year loans, carrying ¾ per cent interest (or service charge) and a ten-year grace period.

In the fall and winter of 1962–63, consequently, in its own interest as well as that of the less developed countries, the United States pressed very hard in the DAC for an endorsement of easier terms of aid. Such an endorsement, it was hoped, would have

[1] *Proceedings of the United Nations Conference on Trade and Development: Final Act and Report,* UN Document E/Conf. 46/141, Vol. I (New York: United Nations, 1964), p. 44.

at least a hortatory effect on several major donors—primarily the Germans, Italians, Japanese, and Canadians. The resultant resolution, adopted by DAC in March 1963, was neither so clear nor so mandatory as its sponsor would have liked; but it did endorse the proposition that the terms of aid ought to be adjusted in the light of the circumstances of the borrower, or, otherwise stated, that, for the most part, increased aid must also be easier aid. The high-level meeting of July 1965 recommended rather specific measures to carry out the resolution, and again urged improvement in aid terms.

Commitment to an increase in the volume and improvement of the terms of aid thus has been and remains the chief doctrinal mandate of the DAC. Other propositions are of course part of the scheme: for example, insistence that aid be an integral part of a total effort involving the developing country as well as the donors. There are factual problems affecting doctrine: questions of absorptive capacity, of concentration of aid, of technique and method. Policy toward tied aid has long been under consideration by the DAC. But problems of volume and of terms, and the resolutions on those subjects, have exercised the principal influence on its *modus operandi*.

Membership

The original members of the Group were Belgium, Canada, France, the Federal Republic of Germany, Italy, Portugal, the United Kingdom, and the United States. To these charter members, Japan was added at the first meeting of the DAG, and the Netherlands at the second. The list of DAC members has grown to fourteen nations (plus the Commission of the European Economic Community) as Norway and Denmark joined in 1962–63, Austria in 1964, and Sweden in 1965. It would seem likely that Switzerland, an OECD member, may find its hesitations about joining DAC, which seem to stem from concern for its neutrality and independence, diminished by the accession of Austria and Sweden, and may apply for membership.

Whether the DAC has been improved by expansion of its membership beyond major donors is debatable. (Portuguese membership has always been considered as something of an anomaly, in view of the nature both of its economy and its program of assistance.) The original proposal envisioned an association of countries able to make "an effective long-term bilateral contribution to the flow of funds," and a number of the more recent members, while providing both technical and capital assistance, do so in an amount which is not great, either in absolute terms or in relation to such measuring rods as gross national product. Some seek, commendably, to avoid the overhead of self-administration (and the political risks of misjudgment or mismanagement) and therefore to entrust grant funds, and sometimes even loan funds, to the management of a qualified international agency. But donors in such categories are not likely to face the problems arising from administering a large bilateral aid program which are the *raison d'être* of the DAC.

Enlargement of the DAC to its present membership has probably not decreased its ability to function effectively—which in this context means for the most part its ability to provide a forum for the frank and knowledgeable exchange of information and ideas. The smaller donors in general speak cogently to the problems of their programs, and to such cooperative efforts as may engage their administrators. The possibility that enlargement of the group could result in its becoming a forum not for the intimate discussion of problems but for the making of the set speeches, which in a number of organizations pass for an exchange of views, seems not to have become a reality. It is conceivable, nevertheless, that the present larger DAC membership does somewhat inhibit the members, and they speak with somewhat more reserve than they would were there fewer. The free flow of associative ideas, the "bull session" on aid actions, problems, new ideas, is more evident in the conversations over coffee or cocktails, when a few of the participants are together, than it is in the formal meetings. To what extent this would be the situation even if the DAC had only five or six members is impossible to say. Since membership in the DAC brings together the discussants in informal as well as formal sessions, enlargement has not impaired the substance of DAC's function of exchanging views. What is probably more important and obviously more difficult in a group larger than five or six is the coordination of "action programs"—what to do in the Congo or Brazil or Tanzania.

Limitation of the DAC to OECD members, and only those which are "donors," means that its growth beyond its present size (with the noted possibility of Swiss accession) is unlikely. There have been some intimations that others might be willing, or in fact desire, to join the club. But its attractiveness has been diminished by the fear of prospective adherents that the DAC commitment to an increase in total developmental aid might imply a specific obligation on the nation applying for membership to enlarge its own aid effort. Despite the understanding, first made explicit with Norway's adherence to the DAC, that new membership involved a commitment to basic DAC doctrine, this fear has not, perhaps unfortunately, had a solid foundation.

It may be that the 1964 United Nations Conference on Trade and Development, with its establishment of aid targets, and the 1965 actions of the DAC have increased the relevance of the general commitment to an increased aid effort to the actions of individual members. Even so, there are several non-OECD nations which would seem plausible candidates for membership. Australia comes to mind. Israel, even while still receiving some concessionary aid, was developing a program, mainly of technical assistance, which has reached impressive proportions. If coordination of, say, the U.S. program with that of Austria is appropriate, why not use the DAC to bring together Americans and Australians, French and Israelis?

There is, in fact, little perceptible reason why this should not be done, other than the deterioration in intimacy which accompanies every increase. Homogeneity is not an obvious characteristic of the programs of DAC members, nor are they, with Japan in the group, geographically unified. But, added to a general reluctance to enlarge the DAC further, there is the relevance of the OECD to DAC functioning. Though the DAC is somewhat apart, it is still a committee of the OECD. Its members participate in the other work of the OECD, a great deal of which is closely relevant to that of DAC. Both the Trade Committee of the OECD and the DAC are concerned with the relationships of trade and aid, to take but one example. The monetary problems discussed elsewhere in the Château de la Muette are integral to the amounts and the terms of the bilateral aid programs. There is thus (despite the apparent historical anomaly of Japan's early membership) good reason for limiting the DAC to OECD members.

Such a limitation need not, however, prevent a close association with like-minded, nonmember donors. Particularly insofar as the DAC functions as a forum for the exchange of information and for discussion of common and general problems—the significance of the growing burden of debt service in the less developed nations, for example—it would seem that countries like Australia, New Zealand, Israel, even Venezuela and Mexico, might be invited to participate. When other problems arise which demand a more direct coordinative effort, *ad hoc* arrangements can always be made.

Procedures

As a natural outgrowth of the process of confrontation which had been the mainstay of OEEC discussion, the DAG early evolved a procedure wherein a description of a donor's program was followed by discussion of that program by the other DAG members. The confessional was at first limited to the government acting as host. By the third meeting, held in Washington in October 1960, the practice was that every delegation, and not only the host, should make a statement about the policies and institutional arrangements of its own aid programs.

This procedure, the forerunner of the present Annual Aid Review, was further formalized at the London meeting, when it was decided to elect a chairman and vice-chairman for the remainder of the life of the DAG. Regularization of the procedure was established at the Tokyo session of July 1961, at which time a Working Group on the Common Aid Effort was set up.[2] This Working Group, under the chairmanship of Ambassador James Riddleberger of the United States, a distinguished career foreign service officer and former director of the U.S. aid agency, was asked to prepare recommendations on: (a) periodic or other reviews of the amount and nature of the aid flowing to the developing countries from DAG members; (b) procedures and documentation for such reviews; and (c) principles to guide the discussion of participation in the common aid effort.

[2] The Tokyo meeting also endorsed the establishment of consortia as a coordinative method. But the vogue for consortia was even at that time on the wane. As already mentioned, consortia carried the implication of a financial commitment; and governments began to have second thoughts about the desirability of such commitments, even if implied, almost immediately after the World Bank organized the consortia for India and Pakistan. The OECD consortia for Greece and Turkey resulted largely from their membership in the OECD (whose charter spoke of economic development), their imminent associations with the EEC, and other special factors.

After the Tokyo meeting, the DAG became the Development Assistance Committee, pursuant to a ministerial resolution of July 1960, which established the lines of procedure for the as yet unborn DAC: its place in the OECD, its competence to select its own chairman, its right to invite representatives of nonmember countries or other international organizations to take part in its discussions, and so forth. The OECD connection also imparted to the DAC the general developmental mandate of the OECD itself. Article I of the OECD Convention states an aim not only to promote growth and stability in member countries but to contribute to sound economic expansion in nonmembers which are in the process of economic development. Article II amplifies this aim by stating that members agree that, individually and jointly, they will contribute to economic development "in particular, by the flow of capital to those [less developed] countries, having regard to the importance to their economies of receiving technical assistance and of securing expanding export markets."

By the time of the first Annual Aid Review in 1962, the DAC had already acquired certain of its present characteristics. It was a relatively small organization, within the context of what one might call the Atlantic Community. Its homogeneity was far from complete (Japan was hardly a part of the "Atlantic Community"), the comparability of the programs was often more statistical than real, and the aims of one member were in many cases not those of another. But, for all that, the members had more common interests than divergencies, were all engaged in the export of capital and technical assistance, and had a similar if not identical confidence in the set of values associated with what may be loosely categorized as free enterprise economies. With some wariness but substantial conviction in its virtues, the members were committed to "coordination" of their aid programs. All believed that progress in the less developed world required external assistance, that they had some kind of obligation to provide a measure of such assistance, that such assistance should increase in amount and should take into account the difficulties which the recipients would have in repayment. The setting up of the DAC affirmed their willingness at least to experiment with an organization within which the problems implicit in these beliefs and this commitment could be regularly and systematically examined.

THE ANNUAL AID REVIEW

A fundamental DAC technique is the Annual Aid Review—the procedure of confrontation, in which the members undergo the scrutiny of their peers. Common standards are used in assessing the various aid programs of the DAC members. The results have been considerable, and by no means limited to a better understanding of each other's programs.

There is nothing compulsory in the Annual Aid Review. The DAC as an organization has no power to command, or even recommend to an individual member that it change its ways, amend its program, or conform to any ideal pattern. Nevertheless, the aid review process is something more than a mere educational discussion. Though the suggestion has sometimes been made that it is hardly more than a seminar, it differs from the usual educational meeting in that it brings together, for mutual discussion and frank criticism (tempered in language but not in substance by the requirements and courtesies of diplomacy), senior and responsible aid officials, the persons who make operating decisions for their own governments.

The method is a simple one. Questionnaires are prepared by the Secretariat, discussed with governmental representatives, and sent to governments. To some extent, this procedure fits all the programs, from those of France to those of Denmark, into the same Procrustean bed. But the process has the benefit of compelling comparisons which might not otherwise be made, and the answers of governments make it easy to detect both similarities and differences. These are sharpened by the analyses and the consequent questions prepared by the Secretariat. Thereafter, on an assigned date (and on the basis of a schedule almost as difficult to work out as that of a baseball league) each member is examined by the entirety of the DAC, with special inquisitorial responsibility being assigned to three members.

The strength of the procedure is that it is both private and informed. Public explanations of aid policy tend to be banal: officials are present not for substantive discussion but to persuade a particular audience. The audience may be friendly or hostile; it is often uninformed. The DAC review, by contrast, is recurrent and expert. It is objective, but always pointed toward testing the will of the donors toward both cooperation and improvement. As a result, it is educative and also influential. As the Annual Aid Review has continued, it has become more sophisticated and less hesitant. Questions have become more probing, platitudes less frequent. Regular attendance has resulted in a collegial atmosphere, with a high level of pertinence, characterized by sharp and relevant, if not always sparkling, discussion. That the review takes place every year makes it possible to perceive trends which a single review might distort, and to see if promises have been kept and if predictions have come true.

The review has had a considerable effect on the attitude of members toward the financing of programs as well as projects. The 1963 review, for example, showed that the predictions of members of an increased flow of development resources had not been accurate. In case after case, the shortfall seemed to rest on a preference for project financing, coupled with a shortage of suitable projects to finance. Backlogs of projects had disappeared. Preparation of projects was taking longer than had been expected. The delay between the appropriation of funds and their actual expenditure was widening. And yet it was clear that the developing nations were in desperate need of funds, largely to keep important segments of their economies in effective operation. The review process may not have changed a fundamental preference of a lender for project as against program lending. But it sharpened comprehension of a problem which was shown to be common to all lenders, promoted discussion of remedies, and led at the least to a broader definition of the term "project"—and a more adequate meeting of development needs —than had previously obtained.

It is, of course, essential to this kind of result that the review be conducted among responsible officials. This is not always easy, such persons generally having a sufficiency of problems to justify their staying home. But the fact that there generally has been a "theme" of current importance during each Annual Aid Review has helped to bring such officials forward, at least in defense of their own programs, and often they remain to join in the interrogative process. Without such a theme, there tends to be a certain deterioration in the level of attendance. The merit of the annual review is regularity; but that same attribute dulls the charm of attendance. And the tendency to schedule special meetings for the urgent issues of the moment sometimes makes it difficult to sustain interest in the regular review.

More questions are asked than answers given in the review sessions. That, however, is not the principal threat to their utility. Rather, it is that they will be regarded as a routine and statistical exercise. Were that to come to be the case, they would lose their chief value—the requirement that one's accepted and often unquestioned beliefs and policies be defended each year in the face of friendly but direct, polite but informed, questioning.

THE ANNUAL "HIGH-LEVEL" MEETING

As immutable a law of international organizations as that of their virtual indestructability is one which prescribes that each year's activities be commemorated in a meeting. That meeting, so the rules go, is to be held at as high a level of officialdom as can be induced to attend. In the Development Assistance Committee this annual meeting flowed somewhat naturally both from the program of meetings in the days of the DAG and from the desire to discuss the problems and the prospects disclosed by means of the Annual Aid Review. The first such meeting of the DAC, held in the summer of 1962, was initially labeled a "ministerial meeting." It promptly became evident that ministers—heads of their various departments or agencies—were not likely to attend; and the annual meeting has since come to be rather inelegantly described as a high-level meeting.

A number of reasons for holding such a meeting may be advanced. In the case of the DAC, it seems evident that responsible policy officials might come together after the total review process has been completed, to analyze and assess, and to make the review process into something more than an academic exercise. Whether this convocation need be on any level other than that implied by the word "responsible" is a somewhat different question.

Clearly, two main lines of purpose can bring top-level officials together. In the one case, there may be substantive issues to be discussed and agreements of substance to be reached. Although the necessity for this kind of consultation will not always await the more or less fixed date of an annual meeting, it is possible that the problem and the meeting will coincide in time, and that the annual meeting, at a top level of officialdom, will thus be amply justified.

A second rationale derives from the absence rather than the

presence of crisis or a specific problem. It is persuasively argued that ministers or their immediate subordinates, engaged in work of a similar type, ought to come together from time to time. In a noncrisis atmosphere, freed from the pressures of daily cable traffic, they can get acquainted with each other and with the problems of each, to the benefit of their mutual objectives. Regularity should of course characterize such meetings.

In some situations, the theory is supported by the fact. The World Bank and International Monetary Fund, for example, do have annual meetings of their governors, who are more often than not ministers of finance, governors of central banks, or the like. And, although many such meetings are centered on an important topic (the revision of Bank policies in 1964, the monetary problems of international liquidity in 1965), often the meetings are attended largely for the corridor conversations, the opportunities to meet one's counterparts informally and quietly in a place where such meetings will excite little or no comment.

In the case of the DAC high-level meetings, the argument of crisis or of calm has, all too often, failed to persuade ministers or their subordinates to leave their desks. The DAC meetings lack the glamour and the prestige of the World Bank and Fund sessions. DAC is itself a part of the OECD, and the OECD has its own ministerial meeting. At the first "ministerial" DAC session in 1962, the United States was represented by the Deputy Administrator of AID—an official whose competence was unquestioned, who had much to do with DAC, but who was not, in the eyes of other members, either a minister or the immediate deputy of one. Nevertheless, that meeting was at a "high level"; but so immediately did it bog down in a morass of pettifogging discussion about publishing some statistical tables (thought by some to present their aid program in an unfairly unfavorable light) that the inevitable result was to discourage future attendance.

Since the disastrous experience of 1962, DAC annual meetings have generally been attended at a reasonable, but not always high, level of officialdom. There is some question as to the necessity for such a meeting. The DAC is, after all, regularly in session, with participation from capitals in most if not all cases. The OECD has its annual meeting. And it has been suggested that the DAC session could with profit be combined with that of the OECD.

An apparent revitalization of the annual DAC meeting did take place in 1965. The 1965 session came at a time when the bilateral donors were faced with growing dissatisfaction on the part of their legislators with aid results, and with the unresolved questions of the donors' relationship to the United Nations Trade and Development Board. There was an intensified appreciation of the mounting problems of debt service in the less developed countries and concern over the unsatisfactory rate of growth in those countries. Pressures for multilateral administration were increasing. The World Bank had, in the previous year, undergone a vigorous re-examination of its own precepts and practices. New administrations had come into office, notably in the United Kingdom. The result was a meeting which was truly high-level (for the first time), which produced perceptible results, and which gave new life to the concept of an annual meeting on a high level of officialdom to consider the development assistance problems of the year. Whereas the institution of the high-level meeting had been threatened with extinction by sentiments of polite indifference or ennui, the 1965 meeting demonstrated that such a session can serve a useful purpose—though whether on a regular, annual basis remains to be proved.

THE CHAIRMAN AND SECRETARIAT

Since the March 1961 meeting of the Development Assistance Group in London, the organization has had a chairman (American) and a vice-chairman (French). For its Secretariat, it relies upon one of the branches—the Development Department—of the OECD Secretariat. By tradition, a senior officer of the Secretariat works closely with the chairman, though remaining theoretically responsible to the secretary-general of the OECD rather than to the chairman.

In the work of the DAC, the chairman and the Secretariat play highly important roles. Both, though acting within the bounds imposed by their responsibility to the totality of the DAC membership, can substantially influence that work. The Secretariat can and does do more than prepare documents and report meetings. Its formulation of the questionnaires on which the Annual Aid Review rests, its summary of each member's reply, and its presentation of written questions can do much to sharpen and to give tone to the aid review. In practice, the Secretariat has been essential to the accomplishments of the DAC. It has been an active participant in the review process. Its inclination has been consistently toward implementation of the agreed policy lines of the common aid effort. Criticized from time to time either for taking a too active or a too passive role, it has always been clearly on the side of an increased and bettered aid effort. Its presence has greatly helped to narrow the often evident gap between preachment and practice.

The chairman, if one may thus depersonalize the two active Americans who have occupied that post, is even more important. His personality naturally influences his role. In the early days of the DAC, the diplomatic skill and light touch of guidance which characterized Ambassador Riddleberger's performance were vital factors in reducing the deep suspicions surrounding the DAC—suspicions, not without foundation, that the United States would attempt to use DAC to press the Europeans to take on a larger share of total aid. In later days, the expertise and substantive knowledge of a former Assistant Secretary of State for Economic Affairs and head of the economics department at a leading American college, Willard Thorp, made it possible to develop a thrust and an orientation which have given the DAC character and influence.

The style of the chairman will of course vary, as will the extent to which he emphasizes his status on the one side as presiding officer or on the other as leader of the group. It seems clear, however, that the pattern has been strongly enough molded so that, provided there is no unanticipated change in the policies of members, he will continue as a semi-independent official, in but not quite of the OECD, capable of leadership in the procedures of the DAC and the policies of its members. His relationship with the secretary-general may at some future date prove troublesome. It has not been so, because of good sense and a shared purpose on both sides.

In the arsenal available to the chairman—the possibilities of proposing special meetings, of commenting during meetings, of opening and summarizing sessions of the DAC, of talking quietly to officials in his office or at home—none is more important than his annual report. The first such report, issued by Chairman Riddleberger in 1962, established the practice of suggesting as well as summarizing. Each of the later reports has had something of a character of its own, depending on the events of the previous year. Each of them has summarized the results of the Annual Aid Review and has sharpened the focus of that review. The 1964 report admirably analyzed problems and suggested approaches to those problems. The 1965 report set the tone, and was in effect the commentary on the agenda for the most productive high-level meeting since the birth of the DAC.

No chairman of the DAC can afford so to sharpen his report as to incur the resentment of a member or members. He cannot favor the views of one member—believe in them though he may

—to the extent of impairing the conviction of his impartiality. He is constrained by his responsibilities as a presiding officer. But, despite all this, he has a body of agreed doctrine to support such efforts as he may make to improve the performance of members, and to achieve the mutuality which is at the core of the common aid effort.

*   *   *

As a self-appointed group of the rich nations of the free world, the DAC might be considered, a priori, to have a divisive and prejudicial influence on relations between rich and poor. But its doctrine from the outset has laid emphasis on increasing and bettering the flow of resources to the less developed nations. Its procedures, guided by Secretariat, chairman, and the more insistent of its members, constitute a continuing reminder of the promise and a goad toward performance. Each year the review process culminates in a published report of the chairman, which summarizes, compares, chides, and exhorts. Doctrine and procedure combine to make it possible for the chairman to act not merely as a presiding officer but as pastor of his flock and keeper of their collective conscience.

In their association in the DAC, members thus emphasize not only their common wealth but their common obligation. They have thus an opportunity to lessen, not widen, the psychological as well as the economic gap which separates the developed from the developing nations of the world.

Chapter IV

Performance of the DAC

Words strain,
Crack and sometimes break, under the burden,
Under the tension, slip, slide, perish,
Decay with imprecision, . . .

T. S. ELIOT*

Measurement of performance in human affairs is difficult, as the what-might-have-been is unknown. The steps taken to implement policies are followed by events. The question of whether these measures have caused the events, wholly or partially, is often unanswerable. Sequence in time does not always demonstrate a causal connection. An always pungent economist, J. K. Galbraith, has in fact argued that quite contrary economic policies have, in the case of countries which have reached a certain level of development, been equally followed by strong economic growth.[1]

It is, consequently, not easy to measure the impact either of the commitment of DAC members to improving the aid effort or of the regular examination of their performance through the

---

* From "Burnt Norton" in *Four Quartets*, copyright 1943, by T. S. Eliot. Reprinted by permission of Harcourt, Brace & World, Inc.

[1] See New York *Herald Tribune*, November 5, 1965.

process of the Annual Aid Review, the chairman's report, and the summation of the annual high-level meeting. After an initial increase in levels of aid, more or less coincident with the beginnings of the DAC, levels of official aid have remained quite static. Would they, if there had been no DAC, have dropped? Terms of aid have improved. Would circumstances in any case have brought about that improvement?

One can nevertheless say, with some degree of certainty, that a better understanding of the programs of aid has been achieved; and one can speculate that understanding has led to a better over-all aid effort. Given its combination of doctrine and procedures, the work of its chairman and Secretariat, and the insistent pressure of certain members—notably, the United States —it seems reasonable to believe that the DAC is at least in part responsible for the gradual improvement of the aid programs of its members which has marked the 1960-65 period.

The aid review analyzes what DAC members are doing and, over the course of the years, whether their programs are on the rise or are materially changing. Consequently, the DAC attempts to examine aid from the point of view of the developing countries. Here there are roughly two ways of proceeding. The members can look at the problems of a particular developing country, or a group of such countries; or they can look at problems common to the development process. The one technique is geographic; the other, functional. In the one, the problems of Turkey or Colombia or Thailand might be considered; in the other, the problems are those of "appropriate" levels of aid, of relationships between aid and performance, of the relevance of debt-service burdens to the efficacy or amount of aid. Obviously, the categories overlap and are meaningful only as a convenient method of organizing work. To that extent, they are useful.

Development, as Maitland said of the law, is a seamless web.

To separate the programs of the donors from the problems of the recipients is sensible, even as a pedagogical device, only if the artificiality and the purpose of the device are kept in mind. For purposes of organizing its work, the DAC has made this separation. On the one side, it has devoted itself to its original tasks, that of comparing aid programs of donors, the process described in the previous chapter. On the other side, it has with some degree of regularity examined the development process primarily from the viewpoint of the recipients of aid. Here it has used both the geographic and the functional approach.

Devising a Geographic Approach

Any attempt at geographic coordination of aid in the DAC raises several threshold questions.

One question is whether the DAC is appropriate for such co-ordination. Can an organization properly undertake such a task if it does not admit to membership, as a matter of right, the countries which are the subjects of the coordination? Or is that something to be done by a group of more general member-ship, like the IBRD, or one with even wider membership, like the United Nations Trade and Development Board?

The second type of question, assuming the DAC as the forum, is that of scope. Should the exchange of information be limited to what each donor is doing, or should it be extended to recom-mendations for the future? Beyond recommendations, ought there be an effort to arrive at agreements, on broad principles or even on specific working arrangements?

As the history of the DAC suggests, its founders considered its jurisdiction to be limited. Its functions were thought to be more those of exchanging information and views than of arriving at any decisions on specific countries. Discussion was to concern ideas, not places; principles, not money. The first DAG meeting, in Washington in 1960, in fact took an explicit decision that efforts to coordinate aid should *not* involve discussion of amounts of financing for individual regions, countries, or projects.

There is more to the background of this restriction than the thought that other institutions were better suited than the DAG for such discussions. The United States had only recently given point to its conviction that others should increase their share of total aid costs by sending its Secretary of the Treasury and Under Secretary of State on a swing around the European circuit to press the argument. Participants in the DAG had a lively apprehension that the organization might become a vehicle for continuing U.S. pressure on other actual or prospective donors. Were that to be the case, the danger, in their eyes, would lie more in the discussion of individual recipient countries and of projects than in general exhortation. The more specific the discussion, the more likely it was to lead to attempts to fix the amount of a bill and to divide it up among the club members. Hence, some of the fears of country discussions.

It was also thought that an adequate forum, the World Bank, already existed for discussing areas, countries, or projects. The Bank was experienced and well staffed. The DAG had no experience and, for the moment, only such staff as could be scraped together out of the remnants of the OEEC. The Bank had funds; the DAG had none. The Bank had made many country studies. The DAG, obviously, had made none, nor was it equipped to make any. The Bank had organized and was leading several consortia. Few were eager either to multiply consortia or to encourage the possible sponsors of consortia. The geographic limitation was thus easily agreed upon at the outset.

In some ways, this restriction has been observed by the DAG and its successor. There have been no consortia organized within the DAC, although the two consortia organized for Greece and Turkey by the OECD would seem to be just about the same thing. And when the DAC has discussed countries or regions, or contemplated discussion of projects, it has avoided the final step of adding up and apportioning a bill.[2] But it has nevertheless violated its original proscription, and has discussed regions and countries and even, to a small extent, projects. It has considered all the matters which lead to a final decision on "how much": what the economic and financial prospects are, what effects the country's politics will have on its economic future, what role external assistance should or could play, and so forth.

One reason for this development is that it is hard to have a sensible conversation about aid policies and programs, and about whether and how they interact upon each other, without talking about a geographic unit. Aid policies do not function in thin air. They affect economies and peoples; they determine import schedules, the pace of industrial expansion, the ability of consumers to fill their stomachs or their coffers. These matters exist somewhere, in a unit of geography. Given the present nation-state organization of the world, the geographic unit generally most convenient for discussion is the country. For some problems, it may be a region of several countries, or a part of one country. Whichever it is, it is hard to prevent some geographic unit from intruding into even the most theoretical discussion of aid policies.

It has not been easy to work out the extent to which the DAC should concern itself with specific country or regional problems and the manner in which it should treat them. Some thought that this role of the DAC should be substantial. Among them were a number of persons, mostly in the United States, who

[2] The DAC did play a role in working out pledges to the United Nations Congo Fund.

acknowledged the pre-eminence of the World Bank in the study of country development problems, yet drew from that acknowledgment the conclusion that another forum, less bankerlike, was needed. The reappraisal of aid and its relation to the Southern Hemisphere which began with the election of President Kennedy exposed many dissatisfactions not only with over-all economic progress but also with the existing instrumentalities of aid. One result of the appraisal was a reshaping of the U.S. aid program, both in doctrine and in administration. A second was a feeling that economic development was too important to be left to the bankers. Another was a conviction that the attainment of economic development required cooperation among the free-world donors, and that the executive directors of the IBRD, stationed in Washington and dealing with the administration of the Bank, were not the most effective channel to national ministries of economy, aid, and finance.

The World Bank, conscious of its need to maintain credit in the Wall Streets of the world, had established a reputation for making sound loans. Critics were now suggesting that it had given too little weight to the requirements of over-all economic and social progress, and that in focusing so much on the soundness of a project it neglected the total forward movement of a less developed country. In itself, a project might fulfill IBRD criteria; but it might widen disparities in income rather than close them. It might contribute little to a country-wide increase in skills and competence. The IBRD was said to approach its loan applications as would a rather benevolent banker, but still a banker interested less in social progress than in the rate of return, the chances of success, and the prospects of repayment.

Such a description of the World Bank's objectives and practices would not go uncontested, and rightly so. Clearly, the Bank was concerned with its reputation for making sound loans; and it was not then prepared to do such atypical things as investing its funds in education. At the same time, any Bank project loan was made within the context of a country study, and was intended to make a sound contribution to over-all economic development. The discipline involved in requiring the borrower to justify projects was a major contribution to the learning process, which was itself indispensable to economic responsibility.[3] The Bank could rightly claim that concern for the general progress of a developing country—not merely the success of the project financed—was always a moving consideration in its lending.

Nevertheless, a feeling, whether well or ill founded and however hard to define, existed in the United States and elsewhere that the institutional arrangements of the Bank could well be supplemented by those of the Development Assistance Committee. To some degree, this sentiment was based on dissatisfaction with the Bank. To some extent, it exploited the view, quietly prevalent among continental Europeans and in less developed countries, that the Bank was an Anglo-American enterprise. It was based much more, however, on a conviction that aid policy was an integral part of the foreign policy of donor states, and that discussion of aid policy toward particular recipients should comprehend the entirety of foreign-policy considerations. The virtue found by many in World Bank administration of development lending funds—namely, that the Bank takes its decisions in an atmosphere removed from politics—was thus thought to be an argument for and not against the DAC, where officials responsible for national policy, and well aware of the political influences behind such policy, could consider their common attitudes toward recipients of aid.

[3] The International Development Association makes soft loans, but it prides itself on applying the same standards of soundness to the projects it finances as does the IBRD itself.

Consequently, with the thought of moving the DAC quickly into a general coordinative role, the United States suggested in early 1962 that the DAC should take up and consider a so-called tray of countries, that is, one developing country in each of the major regions of the less developed world. The suggestion seems to have emerged from the proposal of the United States at the Tokyo DAG meeting that the Group sponsor consortia, from the rejection of this proposal, and from the French countersuggestion that informal, flexible coordinating groups be formed as needed. The purpose was to study each of these countries, to analyze its developmental programs in the broader context of DAC concerns, and to make recommendations designed to speed over-all, balanced development.

The tray-of-countries suggestion foundered almost immediately. The Latin American country in the "tray" was Colombia. The choice seemed logical: a number of DAC members were already making developmental loans there. (So also was the World Bank.) Economic progress in Colombia had been good. A compromise of the political difficulties which had beset that once relatively stable country gave promise of renewed prospects for sound development. Colombia had evidenced a desire for increased aid. Its finance minister had visited a number of European capitals to discuss his country's prospects and needs and to solicit assistance. No formal Colombian consortium existed, nor was the formation of such a consortium likely. Why not, then, form a group within the DAC which, without any specific commitment to funds, could discuss needs and programs and contribute to mutual understanding of problems and prospects?

Despite these arguments, no such group was formed, either for Colombia or for any other country.[4] In the Colombian case

---

[4] An attempt in regard to Tanganyika had been made in the summer and fall of 1961, and got nowhere.

the obstacles were several. Many donors regarded the proposal for a coordinating group as only one small step removed from a financial commitment. Authorship of the suggestion in the United States seemed to be a tip-off to an American hope for increased, non-American contributions. The proposal, moreover, met the undisguised hostility of the World Bank. Its involvement with Colombia had been long and extensive, and it clearly regarded the proposed DAC consultative group as intrusive. In addition, the Bank probably felt that the work of the DAC would not only duplicate its own work on Colombian problems but might lead to recommendations from the DAC on the lending policies of the Bank itself.[5] Finally, the proposal for a consultative group was sponsored by American officials in AID responsible for the problems of coordination and for instructing the American delegation to the DAC; but it had less than enthusiastic support from those in AID in charge of the Alliance for Progress. And this latter side of AID undoubtedly had some of the same reservations as had the Bank about the possible intrusion of the DAC into its own operating responsibilities. In short, the trumpet from Washington sounded an extremely ambivalent blast. The Colombian case therefore was compromised: the DAC was allowed to hold a meeting or two, the subject was effectively

[5] A priori, that the DAC might make recommendations to the Bank, as it might to any other lender, does not seem outrageous if the recommendations were appropriately diplomatic. If it can suggest—or imply—to a bilateral donor, as it has, for example, to Germany and others, that its terms are too hard because of debt-service difficulties of the borrower, the DAC might well (if facts justified it) suggest or imply the same to any other important lender. The Bank, in fact, has substantially changed its lending policies since 1964. The work of the DAC may have influenced that change; but the Bank, with its strong management and its own board of directors, is not likely to take kindly any outside and direct suggestions. Nor, for that matter, does it particularly need them, though there are some who feel that the powerful aroma of righteousness which pervades its corridors might be improved by some fresh air.

referred back to the World Bank, the Bank organized its own consultative group, and there the matter rested.

The result of all this was to start the DAC out, so far as geographic coordination was concerned, on a very uncertain basis. The formation of country or regional coordinating groups seemed outside its mandate, even though the limitation had been largely ignored at the Tokyo DAG meeting. Moreover, such groups, under DAC sponsorship, were either opposed or given a very cold welcome by those with funds, like the World Bank and, within the U.S. government, the regional bureaus of AID. And the DAC had not demonstrated such competence as to justify the suggestion that it had an important contribution to make to the increased efficacy of aid, in whatever region or country of the world. The tray-of-countries experiment was therefore quietly shelved.

As to relations with the IBRD, time and experience have demonstrated that fears about the DAC were exaggerated, and the initial abrasions have healed. Under the chairmanship of Mr. George Woods the Bank has expanded greatly its notion of its role in the development process. It now accepts uses of its funds which earlier would have seemed much too risky—as, for example, putting part of surplus into the International Development Association and giving Bank credits for education. On its side, with experience the DAC has developed a mode of operations which stresses careful cooperation with agencies like the IBRD, on which, in fact, it now relies heavily. As a result, the DAC can take up development problems on a geographic basis, and it can, if it desires, obtain assistance not only from the World Bank but from regional organizations as well.[6]

---

[6] A series of new coordinating groups (led by the IBRD, however) was agreed upon at the 1965 high-level DAC meeting.

REGIONAL MEETINGS

The DAC's first, and most painful, experiment with a regional meeting was a session convoked in early 1962, at the request of the United States, to discuss Latin American development. To say the least, there was inadequate advance preparation. Despite the air of urgency which surrounded the session, the United States left objectives ill-defined or unstated. Presentation of the problems of the region was entirely by the United States and seemed more appropriate to that peculiarly American institution, the gospel meeting, than to a gathering of officials. European sensibilities were largely ignored. The Charter of Punta del Este establishing the Alliance for Progress had postulated an inflow of European private and public capital; but no DAC member (other than the United States) had been present when the Alliance for Progress was debated and set up, had been invited to the Punta del Este meeting, had been consulted about the proposals agreed there, or had participated in the Alliance's conclusion that a substantial amount of non-American external assistance was expected to flow to Latin America. The timing of the call for the Latin American meeting and the manner in which it was organized thus aroused justifiable resentments.

The session succeeded only in communicating the impression that the United States felt Latin America to be a vital part of the developing world, and was somewhat frenetically eager to obtain the financial participation of DAC members in the Alliance. It did not convey to other DAC members any feeling that the Alliance (in particular, the United States) desired any advice or was prepared for DAC participation in its affairs, other than financially. Predictably, other DAC members showed no great inclination to come forward with contributions. Understandably, they were thereafter skeptical about both the purposes and the value of "regional" meetings.

Nevertheless, in the fall of 1962, the United States, with some display of fortitude, suggested that the DAC should hold several regional meetings each year. With the massive indifference if not outright hostility of various DAC members clearly evident, the proposal was put forward carefully and based upon a rationale designed to mitigate unfavorable memories. It was argued that such meetings need not be a random discussion of various regional or local development problems, but could be carefully prepared so as to give the DAC members a clear appreciation of the economic and political situations in a related group of less developed countries. Systematic analysis of this kind could, it was suggested, outline the policies and the needs of the countries under discussion, to the end of sharper analyses by members of their own programs. Such a procedure would valuably supplement the comparison and exchange of information about their programs which was the main thrust of the aid review. And it could give to members a clearer idea than they would otherwise have of what was happening in the developing nations, with attention being focused on the problems or the accomplishments of an area large enough to make comparisons useful and small enough to be a manageable unit for study.

Further, it was suggested, regional meetings of this sort could be followed, as appropriate, with sessions on a single country within the region. The procedure as a whole could thus make it possible for the DAC to organize a systematic study of what was happening in the developing world, to come rationally from the general to the particular, and to utilize consequent conclusions in the formulation of the member's own aid policy and administration.

There was considerable opposition to the proposal. The reasons ranged from recollection of the doleful Latin American experiment, to doubts about the relevance of any "region," to the inevitable fear of taking an unmarked road. But the United States, pressing for an active and meaningful DAC, was willing in this instance to put forward its proposal in advance, to discuss it in small meetings and in the corridors, and to mobilize the persuasive abilities of the American embassies in the DAC capitals in support of the proposal. Moreover, the French proposal at the Tokyo DAG meeting was a precedent of sorts, enabling the United States to argue that it was accepting, adjusting, and amplifying a non-American idea. Finally, the American proposals in the fall of 1962 occupied an otherwise empty field. As there were few alternative suggestions for a 1962-63 DAC agenda,[7] the proposal for a series of experimental regional sessions was adopted.

The first of these regional meetings, held in November 1962, reviewed a group of countries in the Far East. These ranged from success stories like Nationalist China to problem cases like Indonesia and Korea. Exchange of information and views was, in each case, carefully prepared. An individual interested DAC member undertook an initial detailed presentation. Discussion was thereafter focused on the particulars of each of the countries under review. The presentation on Taiwan, for example, emphasized the progress made by that country, indicated no need for increased official aid, but did suggest that DAC member governments might well facilitate attempts by the Nationalist Chinese to obtain developmental private foreign investment. The

[7] It is likely that at the time (late 1962) most members thought of the confrontation process—the Annual Aid Review—as quite enough of an agenda. At any rate, solicitation of proposals for an agenda resulted in little or nothing. Despite a feeling that this was not the best negotiating position, the United States therefore had to propose practically the entire agenda, though advance consultation somewhat mitigated the perils of doing so.

discussion on Korea, in contrast, began with a report on the Korean economy, appraised the political situation, and gave rather detailed consideration to the prospects for regularizing Korean-Japanese relations and settling war-generated claims.

The consensus was that the meeting, though unspectacular, was highly useful. A better understanding of the area, of how the various DAC members regarded it, and of the estimated impact of aid was achieved. The effect of better understanding on aid decisions, which result from a multiplicity of factors, including political relationships, is hard to measure. Nevertheless, understanding of what is happening in a region, or, at the least, of what others whose actions affect that region think is happening, can be helpful to a rational process of decision.

The Far Eastern session proved the utility, limited though it might be, of a well-prepared regional examination. It in fact had a special dividend for DAC members, since it provided valuable groundwork for a meeting, held in July 1963, on the balance of payments problems of Indonesia. That session was in its turn well organized, with a clear sense of direction, and could very well have been a shining example of the DAC's ability to handle difficult political-economic problems. Unhappily for the DAC's chances of thus vividly demonstrating its capabilities —as well as for Indonesia—the agreement of DAC members collapsed under Indonesia's increasing ill-temper with the West and its policy of "confrontation" with the new state of Malaysia.

Later regional meetings have varied greatly in content and in quality. A principal common defect is diffuseness. Proximity does not always breed similarity, and, in any case, the "regions" of the developing world are vast. There are difficulties in a meeting which at once attempts to discuss the differing economic, social, and political problems of El Salvador and Brazil, or of Korea and the Philippines.

Nevertheless, these same difficulties are the converse of one of the principal merits of such meetings—exposing a regional lumping-together of developing nations as the cliché it often is. The regional meetings vividly illustrate that classification by region, often important psychologically as well as in other ways, may cloak important differences and inhibit productive analysis. As a technique of testing out the genuine relevance of regional classifications to the programs of aid, of observing results, and of laying the foundation for more specific work, the regional sessions can prove valuable.

COUNTRY MEETINGS

As has happened, there may be a natural step from the regional meeting to the session built around an individual developing country, or around the common problems of a closely knit group of such countries. It is perhaps in its attempt to deal with development in individual countries that DAC has done its most interesting, if not necessarily most successful, work.

Clearly, to examine in a foreign arena like the DAC the specifics of the policies and prospects of an individual developing country is to venture into a treacherous, politically dangerous field. In the first place, such discussion arouses sensitivities which may lie dormant when the talk is general. It is one thing to study in broad terms, even with illustrations, the over-all problem of debt-service capacity, to point out the growing burden of debt and the possibility that additional loans may contribute to the burden rather than relieve it, and to suggest that corrective steps must be taken by both donors and recipients. It is quite another thing when one talks about a country in its absence, discusses its economics and its politics, and risks the inference that a group of industrialized countries is working out some collective policy toward it. All nations, and perhaps particularly those which have long endured the dominance of the great powers, have highly developed sensibilities in such matters.

Secondly, at least in the DAC, country discussions almost inevitably imply questions of money. Whether current levels of aid are appropriate to the circumstances of the country under discussion is a question that is almost inevitably in mind. Whether or not a conclusion is sought, and whether it be explicit or implicit, the connotations worry members and nonmembers alike. The DAC members are wary that the conclusion might imply a financial commitment. The recipient is sensible of the possibility that the conclusion might be just the opposite. A frank statement analyzing a country's policies and its prospects may leak, confidential though the DAC's proceedings are. Political consequences may follow. The prudent course, therefore, is to avoid talking about an individual country and to keep the conversation safely general.

Finally, if conclusions are agreed, there are troublesome difficulties in carrying them out. If all feel that it would be a mistake to continue programs of aid for a country which, hypothetically, is wasting its resources, then to base a coordinating group on that conclusion would cause a storm of denunciation by the less developed countries in general and by the country in question in particular. If the conclusion is the opposite, that more should be done, the DAC does not have the administrative apparatus or the operating experience to put that conclusion into effect. The World Bank or some similar organization, perhaps a formally organized consortium, can better make detailed studies, assess needs, and do the other things necessary to coordinated and effective action.

Nevertheless, the few meetings which have been held on individual countries have shown the prospects for, as well as the limitations of, country coordination in the DAC. In discussions of particular countries, the generalities of policy pronouncements are brought down to the hard realities of what donors are doing and what results are being achieved. Motives for aid—whether they be humanitarian, political, economic, or other—are tested against specifics. Belief in increasing levels of aid, or in easing terms of aid, is contrasted with what has in fact been done. Formal endorsement of coordination is checked against the multiplicity of programs in a single country, and the stated desire to harmonize against how those programs work in a limited, visible, and meaningful context.

DAC has had several such meetings. In some of these, difficulties have been minimal. A meeting in late 1962, for example, was held on the problems of planning and of local, on-the-spot coordination of aid in Thailand. The Thai meeting was worked out with the participation of Thai officials. The discussion gave opportunity for an exchange of views that was welcomed on both sides. The subsequent establishment of an informal consultative group in Bangkok, in which the Thai government cooperates, has produced some useful results. The chief of these, a compendium of programs classified by priority and by cost, has been useful not only to donors but also in requiring Thai officials themselves to sort out and rationalize their own projects.

The Thai example is perhaps not representative. In Thailand the pace of development has been relatively satisfactory, the problems of donors not immense, and the relations good between Thailand and the nations represented in DAC. A more stringent test comes when neither relations nor problems are easy. The DAC has talked, for example, about the Congo and, as mentioned, about Indonesia. Such countries present DAC members with touchy and difficult questions. Here economic analysis depends largely on political factors. Discussion involves questions of stability, of the politics of the country, of its relations with other countries, of the special interests of a variety of DAC members. For example, Belgium has had, and still has, a very special interest in the Congo. So has the United States, which led the effort to prevent the establishment of a Soviet or Chinese Communist beachhead there. Neither American, Belgian, nor United Nations tactics have been universally acclaimed, even by those who endorse their objectives. Beyond their varying analyses of the political situation, the nations directly interested in the Congo see differently the economic prospects and the appropriate economic response. *Mutatis mutandis,* the same could be said of a country like Indonesia, where the United States, Great Britain, and the Netherlands have at various times all had different views colored by their own experience and by their strategic and political interests. In both cases, events outran agreement.

In such circumstances, agreement to harmonize aid policies is unlikely, and the chief benefit of discussion is likely to be that it may require members, under the compulsion of critical if friendly examination, to rethink their policies—perhaps even to withhold or to limit aid. The meetings nevertheless demonstrated that the DAC could usefully deal with difficult cases, and perhaps had a particular capacity in the situation of a problem country where there are several donors and where political interests are both strong and varying.

That country problems are sufficiently individual to warrant a substantial effort and separate study is attested by the 1965 venture of the World Bank into an extensive program of country coordinating teams. How these will relate to the DAC is not entirely sure, though close collaboration is obviously desirable. That the Bank has boldly extended its previous rather hesitant moves in the direction of country coordination, despite or because of its own and the DAC's experience, is an encouraging indication of willingness to proceed from the customary bland generalities to the particulars required by a country study.

The East African work of the DAC is worth special if brief mention. The attempt was to deal with the common problems of a group of countries with close economic and former political links. It was characterized by limited and defined objectives and careful preparation—the exact opposite of the Latin American meeting of 1962. The result was chiefly to demonstrate that overpreparation for a very limited objective, while probably not harmful, is a poor way to use elaborate coordinative machinery, like that of the DAC. More than one road leads to futility.

The possibility of useful work on East Africa—the new state of Tanganyika, and the soon-to-be-independent territories of Kenya and Uganda—was suggested by the British in 1962, in response to the American tray-of-countries proposal. The subject, problems of local currency financing and technical assistance, was thought to be both manageable and worth attention. No financial commitment was to be asked; the region was well defined not only by the links provided by years of British colonial administration but also by many common institutions, including the same currency. The Scylla of excessive difficulty and the Charybdis of lack of interest being thus avoided, orderly, constructive, and useful discussion could confidently be anticipated.

Preparations for the meeting on East Africa began as early as mid-1962. An expert group was convened by the then DAC Chairman, Ambassador Riddleberger, and as the next careful move a study was proposed. The OECD-DAC Secretariat thereupon prepared study papers. In the fall of 1962 a further session was held to discuss the study. The chairman was then authorized to send it to the East African officials and to invite them to meet with interested members of the DAC, the OECD, and the principal international aid institutions.

The meeting on East Africa was finally held in Paris in July 1963, with impressive representation from East Africa as well as from DAC members. With this background of meticulous preparation within a carefully delimited topic, one would have expected a specific agreement to emerge, at least on measures to increase and better the flow of technical assistance. From this small but significant advance, other steps might then have been taken.

In point of fact, the meeting, lasting the better part of two days, produced very little. Discussion was surprisingly general. The sole tangible product was agreement on terms of reference for continuing consultation. This minimal result did not even bring about further consultation until July 1964, one year later, when for the first time a meeting was held in Nairobi under the 1963 terms of reference. In *its* turn, the Nairobi meeting considered the need for operational and technical personnel and the terms and conditions of service of such personnel. It also received an expression of the willingness of the East African states to study, and later to discuss, their financial problems. Once more, little resulted from the Nairobi meeting other than some arrangements between the East African governments and the OECD Secretariat for producing and discussing these studies. Clearly, the consequences of the exercise were not such as to encourage further similar ventures.

Conclusions based on a few instances are notoriously unsafe. But it seems clear that a norm must be found between the sense of haste and urgency and the accompanying disorganization of the Latin American session, on the one hand, and the meticulous overpreparation, the excessive delimiting of objectives, and the consequent sense of ennui and letdown of the East Africa meeting on the other. Surely the generalities of development economics and politics take root not in the air but in the soil of the countries of Africa or Asia or Latin America. And, just as surely, ways must be found to consider what happens to and what are the prospects for the peoples of these countries—as individuals and as members of a society, whether familial, tribal, or national.

Functional Coordination

Country or regional discussion brings into the DAC a sense of immediacy and relevance to concrete measures. But it has its countervailing difficulties; it tests perhaps too directly the willingness of donors to reduce to specifics their broad commitment to cooperation and coordination; and it involves the political problem of discussing matters close to the policies of the developing nations in a forum not their own. By contrast, discussion of a variety of issues basic to aid policies—volume and terms of aid, for example—touches less directly on national sensibilities and involves less closely the often delicate relationships between individual donors and recipients. Partially for these reasons, the DAC has from the beginning approached country or regional coordination warily, while it has considered as its natural province the more generalized "functional" questions of aid policy. Intergovernmental discussion of aid theory is sometimes questioned in the DAC as engaging that organization in overly theoretical debate. But because theoretical discussion has a less direct effect on aid actions than does consideration of country programs, it is still the least disputed of DAC functions.

That a forum for such debate is useful, if not essential, is apparent. Increasingly, the pace of development and the appropriate or possible role of aid in economic development are subjects of concern. Growth in the developing regions in recent years

varies greatly from country to country; but it is obviously unsatisfactory in the large majority of them,[8] despite the fact that,
for the first time in a period of relative peace, vast sums for
developmental purposes are flowing to these countries in grants,
loans, technical assistance, and private investment.[9] This distres-
singly slow progress is obviously attributable in large part to a
number of causes not within the powers of those who administer
aid programs: increasing populations, unfavorable changes in
the terms of trade between the producers of primary materials
and the sellers of industrial products, increasing availability of
synthetic substitutes for primary products, as well as the inevitable economic tendency of the rich to get rich faster than those
whose margin above subsistence makes saving all but impossible.

For some "developing" countries—a term which in this context
has strongly ironic overtones—it is possible that the near future
could thus bring an actual decrease in production and income
per capita. For most, it means that per capita production and
income will go up at a painfully slow rate. For example, it has
been estimated that India, with a 1961 per capita production of
about $80, may, over a twenty-five-year period, improve that
figure to $150—a move from a starvation to a subsistence level
only. Economists vary in their listing of the important factors,
and in their estimates of aid requirements. Clearly, however, the
share of world exports of the developing countries has decreased
over the last decade; their import requirements tend to rise faster
than their exports and their foreign debt burden escalates
rapidly. These and other gloomy facts suggest a foreign exchange
gap between earnings and requirements which is estimated by

[8] In terms of gross domestic product it is often faster than that of the developed countries, but per capita income remains low. There are, of course,
notable exceptions, Kuwait being the most conspicuous.

[9] On a gross basis. As discussed below, repayment and interest are growing
problems.

the United Nations Secretariat to be on the order of $10 billion or higher in 1970. Other experts would consider this estimate low.

The figures cited above are at most illustrative. Nor should they be taken as indicating that a larger and better flow of capital to the developing countries is a sufficient condition, though it may be a necessary one for their progress. Any set of figures on aid requirements, any set of judgments about the requirements for sustained and satisfactory growth, and any estimates based on such figures or judgments are debatable; often they are the subject of intense controversy. Of the making both of analyses and of formulas for development there is no end. Increased interest and specialization among development economists threaten more to come.

One need be no expert, nor need one choose among the various diagnoses and prescriptions, to realize that the problem of attaining a reasonable rate of growth and of improvement in living standards is not easily solvable, and that many a "developing" country may find its people little or no better off ten years hence than they now are. For some, through a happy combination of circumstances—the existence of natural resources, the qualities of the people, the effective use of foreign aid, a fortuitous or achieved improvement in the terms of trade—there will be good progress. For many others, including some with good prospects, the road will be rough; and cited figures like the IBRD estimate that $3 billion or $4 billion per year might usefully be added to the flow of capital to the less developed nations illustrate but one aspect of that rocky road.

To some extent, perhaps to an important extent, the DAC or some similar instrument of coordination should be involved in ameliorating the evident difficulties. It is obvious that resources fall short of requirements; maximum efficiency in applying such resources as exist and cooperation in increasing and improving the flow of assistance are desiderata squarely within the DAC mandate.

The measures which will have to be taken to achieve a reasonably satisfactory rate of growth in the developing countries are obviously largely beyond the competence, in both the narrow and the broad sense of the word, of the DAC. Questions of domestic fiscal, investment, wage, and price policy are involved. So also are the broadest issues of trade relationships. But, just as obviously, aid and aid policies are a relevant and important part of the equations of growth. How much aid is needed, and how much can effectively be put to work? On what terms and conditions should aid be extended? What can be expected, or demanded, of the developing countries themselves in order to maximize the effects of aid? Questions like these have been the source of much of the work of the DAC and seem likely to be increasingly so.

THE AID "TARGET"

It is no simple matter to define an aid "target," or determine an "appropriate" level of aid. Little real progress has been made toward agreement on levels, though as a result of the United Nations Conference on Trade and Development there is some apparent consensus. Not only the congenitally skeptical will doubt its significance.

Early in DAC history, a target figure of 1 per cent of gross national product was thought to be a reasonable objective; and the United States, in its hortatory role, took the lead to urge that aid contributions be brought both to rough parity among the donors and to that figure. The 1 per cent target was endorsed at the 1964 UNCTAD meeting, where all DAC members approved a somewhat circumscribed resolution,[10] and again at the annual

10 See Chapter III, footnote 1. The UNCTAD definition includes private capital.

high-level DAC meeting of July 1965. At the latter meeting, George D. Woods, President of the World Bank, pointed out, however, that although DAC members had long since endorsed an official assistance target of 1 per cent their long-term capital contributions had remained constant since 1961.[11] In the same period, there had been a rise in the gross national product of the industrialized countries of some 4 to 5 per cent annually, or of about $40 billion per year. The result, said Mr. Woods, was "that the constant amount of net official aid represents a declining percentage of the aid-givers' national income."

Whether such a percentage figure is meaningful has been disputed, as it was at the 1962 high-level meeting of DAC, not least by those whose aid is high in "quality" (for one example, carefully administered grants) although low in ratio to gross national product. Implicit in any statistical measurement is some agreement on what aid in fact is; and on this, DAC members have accepted only the most general of definitions, leaving it to academic economists to argue over the "aid component" of a loan. "Aid" has thus never been precisely defined by the DAC, although for purposes of compiling figures, the extension of public credit maturing in more than five years has generally been considered the criterion for inclusion in "aid" tables.

Various formulas for calculating the assistance component of loans have been suggested. All of them begin with the proposition that a grant of funds is pure aid (inspired though it may be by the expectation of a political return on the investment). At the other end of the spectrum are commercial loans—loans comparable to those made by a private financial institution, which are normal adjuncts to the doing of export business. In between are the loans which offer terms somewhat easier than commercial loans but which otherwise differ widely: in the time of maturity

11 See Appendix Table.

of the loan, the interest rate, the period of grace beyond which payments on interest or principal or both begin, or in the currency of repayment.

Various methods have been suggested for working out a valuation of the aid component in such loans. But neither the DAC nor any other intergovernmental body has concurred on any one. It is difficult to agree on the factors to be fed into the formula— how to judge, for example, the amount of aid involved in "sales" of surplus agricultural products under the United States Public Law 480 program. There is also considerable unwillingness among donors to have their own aid programs measured thus mechanically against a cold arithmetic standard, or, on the other hand, to engage in further divisive argument about the importance of the quality rather than the volume of aid.

The United States has noticeably moderated its initial enthusiasm for the establishment of a 1 per cent of GNP target for aid —a change variously attributed to increased sophistication,[12] recognition of the importance of terms and quality as against arithmetic volume, growing doubts about the effectiveness of large-scale capital assistance or the capacity to absorb such aid in a number of developing countries, and, perhaps not least, an American trend toward slightly smaller allocations of funds for development lending, even while U.S. gross national product is rapidly rising.

If it were agreed that there should be measurement of donor abilities and responsibilities, it could be argued that such mea-

[12] Any such target, for example, tends to neglect the relationship between official aid and private investment. In any case, as UNCTAD itself underlined, the aid requirement may well depend to a considerable extent on the trade policies of the developed nations. Increased or sustained export earnings will of course affect the need for external resources via the aid route. The various "compensatory financing" proposals discussed at UNCTAD and subsequently assume such an effect and measure the appropriate volume of aid by reference to it.

surement ought to be based on a progressive principle, so that countries enjoying a high per capita income would contribute proportionately more than donors with a low per capita income. But it seems debatable whether a target, if it is to be established, should be defined by reference to the abilities, or at least the prosperity—that is, the gross national product and per capita income—of the donors.

Any such criterion postulates a series of hard, and often invidious, judgments. For example, the French show a high ratio of aid to gross national product. This may be regarded, as French public leaders sometimes assert, as showing both a capacity for self-sacrifice on the part of the French and their recognition of their responsibilities as a great civilizing and cultural force. Others may think it exhibits French determination to maintain a useful political and economic link with former French colonies. Or those less kindly inclined may regard it as an attempt to maintain "hegemony" over former dependencies whose economic independence has been incompletely achieved.

Similarly, one might question the American surplus food and fiber program. Is it a generous and useful part of foreign aid, so that in the measuring process it should be included near the head of the list? Or has it been, at least until the surpluses began to disappear, merely an American attempt to deal with a domestic headache?

There is thus, at the threshold of a wealth-of-donors criterion of their aid performance, a problem of agreement on what is to be counted, and to what extent. In any case, the attempt to fix an aid obligation seems likely to produce nothing more satisfactory than the ambiguities of the UNCTAD resolution. The overall capacity of donors to transfer resources, and the manner in which such transfer can be handled, may vary widely between nations with similar gross national products. Wealth has its felt obligations and is certainly relevant to capacity to export skills and capital. But since development rather than expiation of the guilt pangs of the rich is the objective, aid might better reflect (within the rather elastic capacities of the donors) what the less developed nations require for achievement of a reasonable rate of growth and of improvement in the lives of their citizens.

Here, in measuring recipients' needs rather than donors' obligations, definition and the establishment of standards are no less difficult. But at least the test is put on the side of the result and of the effect, not on invidious and often irrelevant comparisons of "obligations" which each will define for himself. Moreover, the factors in the equation seem to relate more to objectively ascertainable facts than does an approach from the side of the donors' obligations.

The various projections of gaps and requirements which have been made are generally based on some assumed target growth rate. One such target, which appears as reasonable as any other, is that made for the Development Decade by the United Nations —5 per cent annual growth in the aggregate and 3 per cent per capita.[13] With this target, analyses have generally proceeded to project the need for additional capital or for additional foreign exchange or both in order that the growth target be met.

That precision is not likely is indicated by the wide range of even these estimates. The UN estimates are, for example, higher by far than those generally made some years earlier. Other experts come to lower projections of foreign exchange requirements, based on different estimates of absorptive capacity, on a more optimistic judgment as to the likely inflow of capital, or on lower calculations of the trade gap. Each type of projected figure is likely to be sharply influenced by variations in the

---

[13] This suggests a continuing 2 per cent rate of population increase, which is itself open to some question.

factors on which its formula is based: for example, use of one formula would mean that if marginal savings ratios are only slightly lower than expected, requirements for foreign exchange might well double.

The concept of an over-all aid target for the developed countries as a whole thus seems of debatable utility. Similarly, if 1 per cent or some other percentage of gross national product is taken as a burden-sharing formula, its utility is questionable. On both sides, the mechanics of making determinations are disputable. Nevertheless, the DAC high-level meeting of 1965 reaffirmed the UNCTAD target, and added that members below that figure should make special efforts to achieve further increases. The matter will probably rest there, at least until the next major confrontation of developed and less developed.

TIED AID

The bulk of bilateral aid is tied to the procurement of goods and services from the donor. Despite long-standing DAC concern with this subject, and despite the likelihood that linking aid and procurement may increase costs to the developing countries and may distort normal or official trade patterns, bilateral aid is likely to remain tied. On this subject, DAC pronunciamentos have been feeble and ineffective. The 1964 report of the DAC chairman stressed the possible evils of tying; the United States (whose Marshall Plan aid was untied, in days of a stronger balance of payments) has responded indirectly by pridefully reporting to the Congress that it is restricting some 85 per cent of American aid to procurement in the United States.

The principal effect of DAC discussion of this subject, other than to provide some outlet for the frustrations of nations for whom foreign trade contributes a major share of national income, like the Dutch and the Belgians, has been to expose some of the facts about tying. One is that formal or legal tying is often not necessary to ensure expenditure in the donor country. "Untied" French aid to its former dependencies supports salaries of French administrators and technicians, and does little to loosen the trade relations between France and the recipient. Likewise, British aid to Malaysia or U.S. aid to Guatemala could probably be untied with no serious effect on trade. If, for example, American suppliers have long dominated a market and have provided its capital equipment, it is unlikely that spare parts will be purchased elsewhere than from the manufacturer of that equipment.

On the other side, it is of interest that formal tying may sometimes be almost as ineffective as, in other cases, it may be unnecessary. The procedures of the Agency for International Development, in Latin America for example, may have more of a cosmetic than a real effect. Argentina (to take one case) may be required to use AID dollars for U.S. procurement. But since it gets the bulk of its dollars (and other foreign exchange) from export earnings, and these are not tied, substitution would seem to be possible. In some situations the power of substitution is of course limited. Necessity, and strong trade relations, may result in the majority of the "free" dollars being spent in the United States, so that the dams and factories get built with tied aid or not at all. But most economies have some degree of flexibility and therefore of potential for substitution, if there is advantage in so doing. And many such economies, including some in which the United States has a large aid program, are traditionally oriented toward European markets and procurement.

It is worth noting that if there are many donors to a recipient, and if they make their largess available for a wide selection of purchases, the harmful effects attributed to tying may be much alleviated. The recipient will not be able to buy, using aid funds, from a nondonor. But it will have a considerable ability, using the variety of currencies available to it and its own trade earnings, to buy where the ordinary criteria of choice (quality, price, time of delivery, usual trade patterns, etc.) would dictate.

The 1965 DAC high-level meeting commended efforts to reduce the scope of aid-tying, and suggested several methods of mitigating the adverse effects of procurement restrictions, such as making the best possible domestic terms available, procurement in less developed countries, and so forth. The net impression is nevertheless not one of a strong spur to positive action by donors; and there is no evidence that practices have materially changed since the 1965 resolution was adopted.

There is little question that aid-tying restricts and directs trade, limits freedom of choice, and makes aid more expensive. It can also engender ill-will between donors as well as among recipients: the existence of a large program of tied aid, particularly if it is based on program lending, can have the effect of driving the exports of another nation out of a traditional market; and this, it is alleged, has happened in countries like Pakistan and India. Its effects can be mitigated and in fact are lessened as more donors, bilateral and international, come on the scene, making more choice available to the recipient. The possibility of such amelioration is fortunate, for the aid programs of at least the major donors owe much of their support to those exporters who believe, correctly or not, that they benefit from aid-tying, and the practice consequently shows few signs of withering away.

MATURITIES; INTEREST RATES; PERIODS OF GRACE

The DAC has made more demonstrable progress in its work on other terms and conditions of aid. In the fall of 1962 it agreed to set up a working group on the relationship of terms of aid to the needs of the developing countries. On April 3, 1963, it adopted a resolution on the subject, recommending that DAC members "relate the terms of aid on a case-by-case basis to the circumstances of each underdeveloped country or group of countries." The resolution also suggested that "a significant degree of comparability" in the terms of their aid should be made the objective "in principle" of the DAC countries.

The DAC resolution noted with concern the rapid increase in the debt-service burden of the developing countries. A growing number of these nations devote an extremely high percentage of their foreign exchange earnings to the service of their external debt. As they increase their borrowing to finance further development, they increase the amount of the mortgage against future earnings and, in many cases, create demand which can only be met by foreign purchases, thereby adding to at least the short-range strain on their balance of payments. The shorter the maturities of these borrowings, the higher the interest rates; and the briefer the period between the borrowing and the commencement of repayment, the more these strains mount. Moreover, the pressures are increased by the tendency of many of the developing nations to borrow for long-term projects on terms which are more appropriate for undertakings which would have a quick, beneficial effect on the balance of payments—or the tendency of exporters of capital goods to grant only relatively short-term credits, generally guaranteed by their governments, for what are really long-term capital projects. The capacity of many countries, a few years hence if not now, to service even existing debt, to say nothing of further loans now being contracted, becomes a matter for serious doubt.

A 1965 AID report emphasizes the peril: "the World Bank has compiled data showing . . . that debt service payments grew from about $800 million in 1956 to $2.9 billion in 1963—an increase of 263 per cent in only seven years. . . . Debt service is projected to grow to $5.2 billion annually in 1970 and to $6.8 billion annually in 1975 if the present average terms on loans are maintained."[14]

Foreign debt of the less developed countries was $10 billion in 1955; it was $30 billion in 1965; it may be $90 billion by 1975. The share of their export earnings devoted to debt service was 3.7 per cent in 1955, 9.1 per cent in 1963, and will be in the neighborhood of 13.6 per cent in 1975. To take one of the most striking cases, were it not for the 1964-65 roll-over of the Turkish debt, by 1970 fully half of Turkey's export earnings would have been required for debt service.[15]

Hard terms aggravate the situation. On typical Export-Import Bank terms (5.5 per cent for thirteen years) and assuming a constant annual flow of new loans, loan repayments exceed Bank outflow in eight years. As a result of previous loans, the Export-Import Bank is thus receiving from Latin America more than it puts in as its share of the United States commitment of $1 billion per year to the Alliance for Progress.

A study prepared by the World Bank and submitted first to the DAC and then in revised form to the UN Conference on Trade and Development points out that no simple formula, including that of the ratio of debt service to earnings, can measure exactly the danger of this increasing pressure. Whether the pressure will force a borrower to default on its external debt

14 See U.S. Agency for International Development, *Study on Loan Terms, Debt Burden and Development* (Washington, April 1965), pp. 7, 14ff.

15 The Turkish consortium dealt with debt falling due over a three-year period. In stretching out that imminent debt, over periods ranging from six to almost forty years for various creditors, it greatly reduced the drain on Turkey's external revenues. If foreign aid comes to Turkey on the basis of ten-year grace periods, some calculations show a possibility of phasing out concessionary aid by 1973 or 1974, with existing and new debt being normally serviced. As a result of the roll-over in the consortium and a rise in export earnings, an estimated $145 million went for amortization and interest payments in 1965, against receipts of some $520 million.

service, or eliminate borrowing for development, or both, depends on many contingencies in addition to its accumulated burden of interest and amortization. The ability to transfer may vary from country to country, the flow of capital may affect capacity to service debt, growth may catch up with or exceed debt-service requirements. Problems—and solutions—may be short-run rather than long-range.

It is nevertheless clear that the peril is very great for most developing countries. Nor has the response seemed always to be appropriate, even for those who most clearly recognize the problem. AID itself points out that under the Marshall Plan 90 percent of United States aid was in the form of grants; the present AID program is 70 per cent loans. U.S. terms for development loans were, in 1961, substantially like IDA terms: forty-year maturities, interest of 0.75 per cent, ten-year periods of grace before repayment of principal began. The 1964 amendments to the Act for International Development set a minimum interest rate of 2.5 per cent, and 1 per cent during the maximum grace period of ten years.

Some progress has been made, however. Concurrently with the DAC Terms of Aid Resolution, some liberalization of terms was announced. For DAC members as a whole, the proportion of new loans with interest rates of 5 per cent or more fell from 70 per cent in 1961 to about 40 per cent in 1962 and 30 per cent in 1963. The proportion of loans at less than 3 per cent rose from 19 to 40 per cent during this same period. Also, repayment periods of official bilateral loans have lengthened. Maturities of twenty years or more in commitments for loans went from about 33 per cent in 1961 to over 50 per cent in 1962 and 1964.[16]

---

[16] See *Development Assistance Efforts and Policies, 1964 Review,* Report of Willard L. Thorp, Chairman of the DAC (Paris: Organization for Economic Cooperation and Development, 1964), pp. 44ff.

In summarizing DAC efforts for 1965 the chairman indicated that:

—Canada is now more liberal than the United States. Its soft loans are for fifty years, at 0.75 per cent interest, with a ten-year grace period.[17]

—Germany has made a few loans at 1 and 2 per cent interest with maturities up to thirty years, with a large share of its development lending being at 3 per cent for twenty-five years with a seven-year grace period.

—The United Kingdom began in 1963 to make the bulk of its loans at twenty-five years, with a seven-year grace period. Since no interest at all is charged during the grace period, the over-all effective interest rate is about 3.5 per cent. (The White Paper of August 3, 1965, previously mentioned, emphasized the British intent to make some interest-free loans.) [18]

Despite this apparent progress, the 1965 AID study points out that on terms of lending commonly used by DAC members, and given a steady annual volume of loans, repayment of principal and interest will equal new lending by the eighth year. Even under favorable conditions it would seem unlikely that many developing countries would be able in so short a time to dispense with a net inflow.

Yet the terms used even by the limited membership of the DAC vary substantially. The United States, the largest donor, makes about 62 per cent of its aid available as grants or something similar, if one includes P.L. 480 sales for local currency (which impose no external obligations on the purchaser). American development loans made in 1963 had an average maturity of thirty-two years, an interest rate of 2 per cent, and grace periods of ten years were granted for more than half of new loans.

17 Although Canadian *development loans* are on this basis, the over-all Canadian program is considerably harder than that of the United States.

18 *1965 Review,* cited, pp. 84-87. This summary of progress gives a far from complete picture.

Despite recent hardening of United States lending, these terms were roughly twice as favorable as the average of other DAC members. Averages, of course, conceal as well as reveal: thus, on the other side, almost 94 per cent of the Norwegian 1963 program was in the form of grants.

The borrower has perhaps the largest stake in obtaining development funds on a basis which does not place an insupportable burden on the future. But lenders are also interested in avoiding defaults. Specifically, that lender whose loans have an maturity date far in the future is desirous that the financial condition of his debtor not be impaired by improvident short- or medium-term borrowing. From his point of view, harmonization of terms is important not merely to the welfare of the borrower but to his own willingness to continue to make long-term loans.

It is unlikely that any major donor will long continue to make long-term soft loans if others are lending to the same recipient at hard terms. In such cases the suspicion exists that the more generous lender is financing not development but repayment of the shorter-term creditor. When this suspicion is added to the demonstrable fact that development can hardly be financed on the basis of hard loans, in view of the arithmetic of the amortization tables, it becomes apparent that harmonization of aid terms has high importance.

For a variety of reasons, some variation is to be expected among donors. Smaller donors will presumably continue to make grants for health, education, and similar purposes, as will private foundations. Some portion of the funds of the major donors will be grants. Special interests will influence the form of aid or the terms of loans. The French will probably continue to make grants to Africa, but not to Pakistan or Turkey. The special relation between the United States and Korea will mean that American aid to Korea will be on terms more favorable than those of other lenders, without too much American complaint.

It is nevertheless the case that if the "mix" of a donor's aid to a particular recipient contains a large percentage of loans, it is sensitive to the provision of funds from another source on harder terms, given similar loan purposes. If one country is lending for developmental purposes on forty-year terms—which it will do only if it regards loans of that length as being required by the borrower's circumstances—it is not likely to be enchanted with another lender's twelve- or fifteen-year maturities for development loans. And this lack of enthusiasm for the quick pay-out of another is sharpened when the limit of debt-service capacity seems to be approaching. Moreover, consortia exist for the large aid consumers, like India, Pakistan, and Turkey, and consortia make comparisons not only inevitable but explicit and sometimes invidious—again heightening discontent with wide disparities in lending terms.

It is thus natural that the DAC has endeavored not only to better but also to harmonize the terms of aid. The 1965 high-level DAC meeting gave a major share of its attention to that subject. It noted the progress made in easing the terms of official loans, but also pointed out the continuing and serious increase in debt-service charges. It therefore added some specifics to the recommendations of the 1963 Terms of Aid Resolution. It recommended that DAC members whose aid is not now at least 70 per cent in the form of grants should try to provide 80 per cent of their total official aid at favorable terms: either grants, or loans with maturities of not less than twenty-five years, interest at 3 per cent or less, and average grace periods of seven years. The DAC further suggested that these terms be extended on as wide a geographic basis as possible, and that the target be attained within three years. The gravity of the problem and the inevitability of comparison give some hope that these recommendations will be put into effect.

SELF-HELP AND CRITERIA OF PERFORMANCE

An inquiry into terms of aid leads logically to appraisal of performance. For it seems obviously not useful to subsidize development if, however great the subsidy, development is not to be attained.

Such an appraisal is not easy. Development assistance often plays only a peripheral role in determining whether a country will or will not make discernible national progress. Many developing nations feel enormously disadvantaged by their colonial past, some with reason. Insufficient or poor resources, lack of trained personnel, the vicissitudes of nature, and the ineptitude of governments may prevent the achievement, with the best of will and effort both domestic and foreign, of an acceptable rise in the standards of life. Rapid increase of population is, in most of the less developed societies, an obvious impediment to a rapid increase in per capita income.

Despite the relevance of the subject to its work, the DAC has therefore not made much progress in measuring the efficacy of aid. The logic of such inquiry is strong, and work in this line is recurrently suggested in or around the DAC; but there are too many unknowns or variables, at least in the present knowledge of the art, to make inquiry into the general problem of the efficacy of aid, as a general matter, likely to yield results.

What the DAC can do, however, is to isolate and study certain of the items within the larger problem of efficacy. Some of these (amounts and terms of aid, for example) have already been mentioned. But there are also questions of performance. To what extent are the developing countries helping themselves? To what extent are they usefully exploring outside and domestic resources? What can reasonably be expected of them?

Only recently has the DAC begun to move into this area of inquiry, with its overtones of censorious judgment of the policies and abilities of the developing countries. DAC consideration was somewhat encouraged by a resolution passed by the 1964 UN Conference on Trade and Development, which, in the general terms that inevitably find their way into resolutions accepted without dissent by a multitude of countries of differing views, expressed the concern of developed and less developed alike with performance. Thus the DAC now has a working party on assistance requirements, which has recently completed a report on performance considerations.

In American jargon, this would seem to be the self-help criterion of aid. The United States has led in enunciating the necessary relevance of self-help to the performance of the donors, though there are those—in and out of Congress—who suspect that it has not been in the forefront of enforcing the concept. It has, however, pushed the idea that self-help is the most important ingredient of success in the struggle for economic progress, and that it should be a prerequisite for aid.

In recent years the gap between words and actions would seem significantly to have narrowed. Multilateral deliberation, whether in the DAC or in consortia or coordinating groups, has helped. A multilateral coordinating arrangement, with its analysis of progress made or targets missed, emphasizes the importance of self-help and of effective domestic policies and administration, and stresses the relationship of domestic action to effective external assistance. The relevance of domestic policies is clear when consortium members attempt to estimate the need of the recipient country for external assistance. The point is made somewhat less pungently, but perhaps also more dispassionately, in the more general discussions of the DAC.

To state that self-help is essential is obviously only to open the discussion. What may be expected of Greece may not be possible in Gabon. Lack of skills may render a great effort ineffective. Measurable improvement in performance may represent but a fraction of what could reasonably be expected. The formulation of standards is a formidable task, to say nothing of forging a consensus on them. Even if standards can be stated and accepted, they are likely to have practical meaning only as applied to the circumstances of an individual country.

Here, as in other cases, the DAC is only one of several agencies for carrying on what must be a dialogue among donors, and between donors and recipients. It is likely to move forward somewhat tentatively. Other agencies—IBRD, IMF, the Inter-American Committee of the Alliance for Progress (CIAP), the new UN Trade and Development Board—are all involved in the evaluation of performance on the one side and requirements on the other. Given the nature of the problem and of the DAC, no great leaps forward are to be expected. But the pressures of public opinion and of legislative interest in the donor countries make it clear that criteria of performance will be a frequent topic on many a future DAC agenda. Indeed, the present cautious foray into the morass of evaluating the efficacy of aid may open up the next major field of inquiry for the DAC.

Chapter V

Assessment, Prospects, and Proposals

1. *Assessment*

> They who set themselves to give precepts must of
> course regard themselves as possessed of greater skill
> than those to whom they prescribe.
>
> DESCARTES, *Discourse on Method*

In the tranquil halls of the Château de la Muette a flood of
words about aid has poured forth. Among the recurrent phrases,
none has more consistently been heard than affirmation of the
desirability of coordination of aid, of cooperation among the
industrialized countries which are members of the DAC, of cooperation between these countries and those which are described
as less developed, or developing, or, as the French cautiously
phrase it, on the way toward development. All governments
agree that it is better to coordinate than not to do so, except in
the context of the East-West conflict, where a certain uneasiness
exists, and that the achievement of more coordination and cooperation would enhance the efficacy of aid, to the benefit of
both donors and recipients.

Such doubts as governments may have they do not express in
their official statements. The DAC has several times formally

reaffirmed the continuing validity of the concept of coordination. Similarly, it has underlined in its work and its recommendations the fact that, if it is a club of the rich, it is a club of nations conscious of the responsibilities of the well-to-do toward the less fortunate.

As we have seen, the results of coordination through the DAC have been limited; and there is some undercurrent of doubt among the members themselves whether its achievements will be more tangible in the future. Mainly, the difficulties lie in the likelihood that agreement will be general, while difference is specific. The broad DAC resolutions on the common aid effort, on volume, and on terms show a common concern for a more rapid pace of development. That concern, expressed in the out-pouring by the Western nations of some $55 billions of various sorts of aid since the end of World War II, is based both on humanitarian considerations and on the conviction that im-provement in the lot of the less developed nations is vital to the preservation of a free and peaceful society of nations. But there are other motives for aid, and other backgrounds; and the variety of national motives, objectives, and traditions which lie behind each donor's program may substantially limit the discernible results of the coordinative effort. It is only realistic to take account of those limitations in any assessment of what the DAC has done or can do.

LIMITATIONS

No one national aid program is precisely like any other. But the main differences are between that of the United States and those of the other Western states. In amount, even on the re-duced scale of recent years, the American program is by far the largest. In scope, the United States program is world-wide, though in some cases it is limited to a "presence." Thus, as far as the prospects for coordination are concerned, American policy and the American program have a central place.

The United States, certainly in the countries in which it concentrates, can properly regard its aid as a substantial element in the recipient's development plans. It therefore tends to regard such aid in the context of over-all development and to place importance on planning, self-help, and measures relevant to economic growth. Donors whose programs are not large enough to give them the possibility of influencing over-all growth by their aid tend to give more attention to the specifics of a project. Whether the economy of Turkey will flourish can hardly be determined by the contribution of Austria to the Turkish consortium, and Austria may well be more interested in whether a project which it is financing will be soundly built and will operate successfully than in over-all Turkish planning.

In method, the United States has had enormous surpluses of food and fiber, which it used lavishly in its aid programs. Other donors cannot do this, and some tend to look askance at such aid as likely to inhibit food and fiber production in the developing country, as well as its possible purchases elsewhere. In the matter of terms, the United States has consistently urged either grants or longer and softer loans.[1] Other donors, facing the same facts, feel that loans are better than grants in keeping recipients closer to a sense of responsibility, and that "excessively long maturities" for loans are less desirable than periodic reviews, which may result in a roll-over of external debt, if relief is needed. Even in administration there are notable differences among the bilateral aid programs: the United States maintains large aid missions abroad; the British and French tend to rely

[1] This continues to be the case, even though United States terms were substantially "hardened" in 1963 and 1964, and the proportion of loans in the total program has been rising for a decade.

much more on officials of the recipient government.

Such differences as these may seem more an argument for coordination than a necessary limit on the extent to which donors will cooperate. But differences in techniques, in methods, and in size of the programs do not reflect merely differences in national temperament, or in the gross national product of the donors. They reflect also differences in objectives, and some conflicts in those objectives. Differences of this sort have always afflicted relations between the friendliest of nations, and it is not surprising that there might be such differences in relation to aid. Regrettably, where there are such conflicts, coordination is likely to be celebrated more in the word than in the deed.

"Better geographic distribution" of aid is another good example of an accepted phrase and a neglected objective. The United States has long argued for a "better" distribution of aid. This could mean that each donor country should undertake a more equitable distribution of its own funds, even if all donors retained areas of concentration or specialization. What it actually means, when members of the DAC get down to specifics, is that several of them consider the French program to be too highly concentrated in an area of limited population, the French-language community of Africa. The French, on the other hand, have shown little inclination to scatter their largess more widely. The Jeanneney report has suggested a broadening of the French program, and some gestures—including a substantial extension of export credits mixed with governmental guarantees to Mexico—have been made toward Latin America. But, despite urging in the DAC, a significant shift in the pattern is not likely.

Moreover, the principal donor in a region may well regard the geographic expansion of the aid programs of others with something less than enthusiasm. The cultural "mission" of the French in Latin America will probably cause few cheers in Washington, which may welcome such French help there with the same warmth with which it greets French policy toward Southeast Asia. Conversely, the existence of a large American aid program in countries which have recently expropriated French holdings will have about the same reception at the Quai d'Orsay as would a similar French program in a country to which the United States had cut off aid. As the DAC chairman has somewhat gingerly pointed out, each of the developing countries would wish itself not to be entirely dependent on the former metropole, or upon its chief trading partner;[2] but the opening of windows to wider vistas may not be wholeheartedly and universally cheered.

It is, of course, graceless to suggest that one donor would not be pleased to see another enter its "sphere of influence," to use an old-fashioned and unpopular phrase. (And DAC discussion is polite for entirely useful, as well as proper, reasons.) The United States has, in fact, made several somewhat schizophrenic attempts to get more European and Japanese long-term soft money into Latin America.[3] But, at least at the earlier of the presentations, even a reasonably sympathetic observer might have had the impression that it was only funds, not advice or participation in administering the program, that would be appreciated. In other areas a similar hesitance probably exists on the part of other major donors in regard to the American aid program.

Frank and lively discussion in the DAC, as in any such forum,

2 *1964 Review,* cited, p. 41.

3 Several formal and informal sessions in Latin American developmental problems were held in the DAC in 1962 and 1963, at which the desire for financial assistance and the reluctance to admit "foreign" influence were equally evident. In later meetings dealing, for example, with the Inter-American Committee for the Alliance for Progress (CIAP) or the Inter-American Development Bank, the reluctance has largely disappeared.

is difficult if it touches a special political relationship between donor and recipient. Economic sensitivities also tend to inhibit the fine free flow of discussion and the pleasure of agreement. It is a simple sequence: bilateral aid results in exports; trade follows aid; and the commercial objectives of the donors come into competition.

To take an example: The German aid effort has been described by Minister of Cooperation Scheel as "welfare policy on an international scale." No doubt the description fits the facts—in part. Doubtless, also, there are other motives for German aid—such as enforcement of the Hallstein doctrine, which is intended to keep the East German regime in diplomatic isolation. Most observers, in describing the German program of aid, stress the desire to promote exports now and in the future and thus to achieve a happy merger of humanitarianism, immediate sales, and long-term commercial and political relations. Other considerations may loom larger in other aid programs; but industrialists, in any one of the major donors, can hardly be blamed for putting some stress on capital goods exports and the future trade aspects of aid.

It is clear, at least for the present as we have seen, that if the Germans finance a steel mill in Peru, they will also build it, and that an American or French or British manufacturer will not get the order. This is well understood, and complaints based on the reluctance of one country to finance the exports of another are rare (except among the smaller industrialized countries who live by external trade, and whose voice on these matters tends to be drowned out by the thunder of the giants). There are some complaints that tied program loans unfairly divert normal channels of trade, and suggestions that they could be so administered as not to do so. At bottom, however, competition in export promotion is accepted as a concomitant of aid. And such complaints as there are tend to be directed to the national governmental unit financing export credits, which uniformly in all countries is accused by its own exporters of making available to them facilities considerably less favorable than those made available by comparable foreign agencies to their exporters.

The coordinative mission of the DAC is thus complicated not merely by differences in the national objectives which lie behind the bilateral aid programs (as well as behind contributions to international programs) but also by conflicts created by or inherent in the aid programs. Recognition that these conflicts ought to be minimized is, nonetheless, shared by the donors. It is not entirely clear that it is shared by the recipients of aid.[4]

At least publicly, the developing countries have expressed little concern about the "rich man's club" aspect of the DAC. On the other hand, they have made little effort to take advantage of the opportunity offered by the DAC for laying their case before those who dispose of development funds.

This disinclination flows partly from the nature of the DAC and its evident inability to make the decisions which such petitioners would desire. But it flows also from a shrewd realization that aid programs rest on judgments as to national interest, and from a feeling that the relevance of aid to a nation's interest can be better argued bilaterally than in a forum in which many nations participate. An appeal to a single government for funds can emphasize political ties, past or future; can point out the potential in exports which a generous loan will enhance; or

[4] The possible, and probably overrated, public relations problem of the DAC being a cabal, or a "rich man's club," is certainly diminished by the formal organization of the less developed at the United Nations Conference on Trade and Development; and it is commonly now said that the less developed wish that the more developed would do a better job of agreeing on a joint position. Nevertheless, economic strength still lies with the developed; and one may question that a strong prefabricated position of DAC members in opposition to projects of the less developed would in fact be welcomed.

can underscore the mutual profitability of expanded economic intercourse. Such a pointed presentation in the DAC would be inappropriate. What is more relevant, it would not be productive. The appeal is therefore not made in the DAC, but in the places where aid decisions can be taken. What the prospective borrower desires above all is not coordination, even within the framework of the common aid effort, but a prompt decision to make new loans and grants.

To the country whose appeal for aid is under consideration and whose affairs are under scrutiny, coordination by the DAC may also be somewhat suspect. The analysis and discussions implicit in a coordinative exercise are likely to stress the uncertainties of a development program as much as its progress and its promise. Within some of the consortia stress has been as much on the need for economic and fiscal reforms in the developing country as on its need for external assistance. Past failures and possible future difficulties are likely to be embarrassingly emphasized. Successes may be thought to suggest a diminishing rather than an expanding flow of aid: thus it is proudly pointed out by AID that Greece, Israel, and Taiwan no longer need concessionary financial assistance. (The pride is undoubtedly shared by these countries; but they might wish that it had other consequences.) The DAC, though it has not aroused the hostility once thought possible or probable, is not necessarily a congenial forum to the borrower, even though the conclave of bankers has proclaimed its benevolent desire to help and has, in fact, done much to prove that desire. And, doubtless, a bit of competition if not confusion among the donors is thought to be an excellent stimulant to maintaining the flow of aid funds from each of them.

Nor has the DAC produced sufficient results, in the few country-coordinating activities it has undertaken, to inspire a rush of applicants, eager to lay their cases before it. Success in increasing the flow of funds to a developing country, or significantly improving the terms on which it received its aid, might have overcome the natural reluctance to come before what may seem distastefully similar to a creditors' committee. But the exhortations of the DAC in respect of volume and terms of aid, which have in fact materially benefited the most disadvantaged among the recipients, have been, in a sense, unfocused. The causal connections between discussion of a developing country in the DAC and an increased flow of aid to that country is, in the words of the Scottish verdict, not proved.

Perhaps through bad luck, as in the case of Indonesia, there are no vivid illustrations of the DAC's ability to help an individual developing nation. Its best instance remains Thailand, where results were useful, but only mildly so. The coordinating committee which met in Bangkok had to be prodded to convene regularly. The laboring oar in the committee was carried by one or two members. The principal result was merely a compendium of projects, with assigned priorities, which was produced by the Thai government. The main visible benefit of the DAC-Thai cooperation was the setting up of a consultative mechanism within the Thai government. So far as is known, no quantitative or qualitative evaluation of the flow of aid before and after establishment of the committee, or after production of the compendium, has been made. Regular discussion of the programs of the bilateral donors among themselves, and with the Thai government, is assumed to be useful, but its actual effect on economic development in Thailand is not demonstrated.

The experience with the less developed countries raises the question of the proper and best role of the DAC. On the one side, it is evident that it can be a major catalyst of discussion, and hopefully of reconciliation of policy, among the donors.

On the other, although a certain feeling of unease colors discussion among the rich of the problems of the poor, there has always been some yearning in the DAC for a window to the less developed world. As its history shows, the DAC has thought it useful, from time to time, to deal with those nations directly.

Achievement here is not great. The fault probably lies in the DAC capitals, in differences among the aid administrators, perhaps in their reluctance to attempt seriously to reach operating agreement, rather than in malfunctioning of the Paris mechanism. Yet the record is not such as to suggest that the developing nations will seize upon the DAC for the purpose of exposing to it their plans, their problems, their needs, and their hopes.

The establishment of the United Nations Trade and Development Board, in which the developing nations will have a large voice, and in which discussion can be expanded more easily into trade matters than it can in the DAC, will very likely diminish such desire as might exist to come to the DAC. The fact that "decision-makers" are in national capitals rather than in delegates' chairs at the Château de la Muette will also draw custom to the chanceries and not to the DAC.

In any contention for honors as a forum for the coordination of aid, the DAC is limited by the less than adventurous attitude of its members toward expansion of its role. It is also circumscribed by the existence of other international organizations which do at least a part of the coordinating job, and generally do it as donor as well as coordinator.

To a considerable extent, and without assuming the role of the coordinator of bilateral aid programs, the IBRD does in fact coordinate. Unlike the DAC, the Bank has always assumed that study ought to be concentrated on country problems. It has consequently made studies of a great many developing countries. These studies, analytic and comprehensive, experienced and competent, not only describe a country's prospects and priorities, but also often contain recommendations which the Bank can back up with its own cash. Its decisions on specific loans are generally buttressed by a substantial additional country study made by the Bank staff, with the cooperation of the country being studied. For the borrower, therefore, an interest expressed by the IBRD holds the promise not merely of advice but of cash to give substance to the advice. Moreover, the existence of not only the Bank but others of its family—the soft-loan IDA and the investment banking International Finance Corporation —means great flexibility in how the funds may be made available. For the donors, their bilateral lending is likely to lean on the findings of the Bank's studies, with their emphasis on nonpolitical and dispassionate economic analysis. It is notable that the DAC has itself come to regard country studies as a particular specialty of the Bank. And the 1965 high-level meeting, having decided that more country-coordinating groups would be desirable, assigned the principal role in forming such groups to the IBRD.

The role of coordinator is, in one respect or another, played by a welter of other organizations as well. The United Nations has its resident representatives stationed in most of the larger developing nations, who attempt at least some rationalizing role among the congeries of UN organizations having something to do with development—FAO, WHO, UNESCO, etc. The UN Special Fund and Expanded Program of Technical Assistance (now combined) are also in the act. So are the UN regional economic commissions for Latin America, for Africa, and for Asia and the Far East. The regional banks are assuming a coordinative role: the Inter-American Development Bank has experimented, with stated success, with a coordinative project for aid to Ecuador. The Asian Development Bank has strong U.S. support, and will administer healthy amounts of American, Japanese, and (it is hoped) European funds.

In Latin America there is coordinative machinery so abundant and complex as to suggest that it is itself in some need of rationalization. Within the latitudinarian confines of the Charter of the Organization of American States, the documents of Punta del Este and Rio de Janeiro and Bogotá, there exists an elaborate set of institutions for ensuring coordination in the interest of social and economic development. As an example of interlocking and overlapping bureaucracy, the apparatus is wondrous to behold; but it seems, particularly since having been capped by the Inter-American Committee for the Alliance for Progress (CIAP), to work reasonably well.

What is sure, then, is that there exists at present no lack of places in which mutual problems of development can be discussed. In many of these, discussion is the more attractive because funds are available to argue the matter of recommendations. And that is an argument not generally available to the DAC, though it is, of course, to the DAC members.

STRENGTHS

In these circumstances it is perhaps surprising that the DAC has done as well as it has and has reasonable prospects. The fact is, it has strengths which are the obverse of its weaknesses.

Limited membership, for example, which prevents its speaking for as well as to the developing nations, has nevertheless promoted an explicitness which, despite many a deadly dull session, from time to time does break through the predictably standard phrases with refreshing frankness. Delegates can, if they wish, talk rather than make speeches for the record. Every action need not be asserted to be based on an almost unearthly humanitarianism. In the DAC it is assumed, as well as often stated, that bilateral (and multilateral) aid will reflect bilateral and often conflicting foreign policies. One can mention, without being charged with abandoning the humanitarian basis which also powerfully motivates aid, that without their export promotion aspect bilateral aid programs would lose most of their domestic support. The limited membership of the DAC often helps rather than hinders.

It would be misleading to suggest that diplomatic caution is thrown out the long windows. After all, rivalries exist among members, policy differences are evident, a careless phrase may be turned back on the phrasemaker. But, in general, what is said in the closed DAC sessions can be designed to make sense rather than, as is too often the case in many an international forum, to avoid giving offense. As a sort of club, the DAC promotes the easy communication characteristic of those who speak the same language, have similar points of view, have known each other for a long time, and can discuss their differences familiarly and in relative privacy. Long preliminaries, self-serving banalities, the platitudinous repetitions characteristic of too many international meetings, drafted more to placate an insistent majority or some public audience outside the conference hall than to illuminate problems or define policy, are here inappropriate. If they occur, they tend to be regarded as embarrassing gaucheries. True, the business which can be done is limited by its being more a meeting place than an organization, by the absence of those whose affairs are being discussed, and even by the hesitancy of its own members about subjecting their aid policies to the informed criticism of others. But when the DAC does do the kind of business for which this assemblage is suited, it can at least talk sense.

What the results of such talk are depends chiefly on whether its members allow the DAC to take on the issues that divide its members. For the heart of such strength as the DAC has is this: it can, in a familiar and reasonably secure atmosphere, discuss frankly the questions of policy or of practice on which members have differing views. Whether it will do so is a critical question. If it schedules the easy and the noncontroversial for discussion—the desirability of increasing technical assistance to East Africa, for example—in an attempt to improve its batting average of recommendations agreed upon, it attempts nothing that cannot be done better elsewhere. Limited membership accords an opportunity, but the opportunity is nothing if it is not recognized and exploited.

The DAC's usefulness, perhaps its unique usefulness, lies in its ability to discuss, in quiet and in confidence, meaningful problems of program or policy. What are "appropriate" amounts of aid or "appropriate" terms of aid, not in general but in the specifics of the programs of the United States, Germany, Canada, Belgium? How important is it that terms vary widely among major donors? Are the variations here in the generosity of donors, or in their capabilities, or in the political or economic bases of their aid programs? What is the amount of aid which should, in the circumstances of an individual donor, be allocated to international administration? Is there a factually demonstrable need for an increased flow of aid, for a changed geographic distribution, for changes in method? The DAC can, if it will, bring together the competent persons to talk to each other frankly about hard issues—aid to Viet-Nam or Korea or the United Arab Republic, or the desirability of a concerted attack on the debt-service burden of Brazil, or assistance at a time of political crisis to a nascent Asian Development Bank— issues on which concert ought to be as specific as it can be, issues posing problems not of aid but of foreign policy.

The differences in objectives and in points of view of governments, we have pointed out, result from the fact that each of them is using its own public resources in accordance with its own concept of its national interests. Reconciliation of differences may therefore often be impossible. But that conclusion, if valid, should be proved in terms of particulars. The DAC can do a great deal to identify issues, to minimize harmful conflicts, and, from time to time, to achieve a coordinated and fruitful approach to their solution.

Where this ability to deal privately with specifics seems most relevant—and least used—is in regard to country or regional coordination. If the DAC assumed greater responsibilities of this sort, it might find itself suddenly attractive to the developing nations. The development authorities of the country seeking increased aid will do well to go to the capitals of prospective donors; but they may also find that an approach via DAC can usefully supplement, and perhaps improve, the chances of the bilateral approach. The DAC stands publicly committed to an increased and improved flow of aid. It is a standing group, with considerable expertise, and with the ability to draw decision-makers—or decision-influencers—from the capital cities of the members. Perhaps curiously, there is in the DAC a sense of group involvement, a sort of team spirit, that can on occasion help toward realization of the objectives memorialized in the basic resolutions.

Despite the cool rationality of diplomacy, a well-argued statement to a group such as the DAC can have a considerable effect. The delegate from a developing nation can have the assistance of those among the DAC members who are his backers. At the Trade and Development Board he is one among many; at the DAC he will hold center stage. In corridors and at cocktails he can discuss his country's problems with delegates from the wealthy nations, all of whom have at least that degree of sympathy implied in their jobs and in the declared purposes of the DAC. Circumstances are favorable. The chairman, the Secretariat, and at least some of the members are probably on the side of some increase of aid. At least as a supplement to presentation in capitals, those developing nations which can make a reasonably appealing case may find in the "rich man's club" a sympathetic and useful audience.

*   *   *

A review of DAC experience yields few explicit conclusions. Demonstrable successes are few, but influence on aid policy and practice is more than probable. The Annual Aid Review gives members a better understanding of each other's programs, and an opportunity to argue for change; the measure of its effect is uncertain, though again it can hardly be other than helpful. The suggestions of the DAC on amounts of aid, on terms, and on criteria of performance should add weight to the many voices that argue for more aid, for better aid, for closer integration of aid with the performance of the developing countries. But this proposition is still only a probability, not a proven reality. Coordination in the DAC has produced some good results, but the most likely successes were stillborn.

There is an observable rise and fall in the pace of the DAC. Most conspicuously, a lull seems to occur after a surge of forward motion which from time to time takes place, as at the high-level meeting of 1965. The program presented by the DAC to the Council of the OECD in November 1965 was a faint echo of the strong resolutions enacted a few months earlier. Between the word and the action—between the high-level meeting with its emphasis on the large requirements, the broad remedies, the necessities of statecraft, and the later working session with its concern for budgets and commitments, its suspicions, and its roots in bureaucracies—there is all too often a vast gulf. It is thus possible for a new British minister to press for vigorous and concerted action, and for a British representative, a few months later, to point out the difficulties of any specific proposals which may be presented as responsive to that pressure. No delegation is unique in this respect. Most, at one time or another, on one subject or another, see all too clearly the imperfections in anything that brings the generalities down to action.

That this is so should occasion neither surprise nor undue distress, provided that the problem is recognized and progress toward its solution is made. The fault lies not in the DAC but in its stars. The achievement by a group of nations not merely of resolutions bravely speaking of worthy objectives but also of actions responding to those resolutions is complex and difficult. Within each program a multiplicity of often conflicting forces exists. Aid administrators favor effective aid programs; finance ministers tend to think dourly of budgets, taxes, trade balances; foreign offices are inclined to regard aid as a political rather than a developmental instrument. The result, reflected in the mirror of the DAC, is likely to be no clear, shining, unitary image.

The image of other organizations is, on the whole, clearer. But the task of the World Bank—the contrast most often drawn —is, without derogation to that excellent institution, much easier, and the results are infinitely more susceptible of measurement. The Bank studies, investigates, makes loans. Its success can be ascertained: one consults its balance sheet, its figure of loans outstanding and of funds borrowed, its reports of projects financed and repayments made, and one arrives at an entirely correct conclusion of useful activity. Beyond this are the extra dividends: its leadership of consortia, its hortatory role, its influence toward responsible economic policy, its cooperation with its sister institution, the International Monetary Fund, on matters of financial policy.

Neither the individual aid administrator nor the DAC can enjoy this clarity of purpose, this possibility of measurement. The bilateral programs respond to domestic pressures as well as to foreign needs; the success stories are relatively few, the attribution of their success difficult. The accomplishment of the DAC lies in actions taken in London or Bonn or Washington, or perhaps in decisions not taken; but it is hard to say what has been the influence of an aid review or DAC resolution, what would in any case have been done, what benefits have resulted or what horrors have been averted.

Thus it is that the description of such concepts as coordination is a deductive and illustrative process—an admittedly imperfect and unsatisfactory method of arriving at an explicit, universally valid definition. Thus, also, the backing and filling of the DAC, and inability to draw up its profit and loss statement, are to be understood in terms of the problem with which it deals, not of the institution—or at least not entirely of the institution. The collaborative effort represented in the DAC is genuine, though often insufficiently specific. It has the benefit of centripetal forces which favor coordination, and it also has to cope with centrifugal forces which make that task difficult. Within such limits as those imposed by the circumstances and needs of the developing nations themselves and within an entirely sincere adherence to the principles of the common aid effort, there is ample scope for differences of opinion or of policy.

It is this combination of differences and common interest that, in fact, makes it possible to attribute a certain importance to the DAC, or, more broadly, to the frustrating attempt to achieve a coordinated attack by the bilateral donors on the harassing problems of economic development. The role of the DAC is thus reflected both in the high-mindedness and in the parochialism of the bilateral aid programs, in the many influences that bear on the expenditure by the donors of billions of dollars. If harmonization were easy to achieve, an institution like the DAC would be of small importance. It is precisely because the task is both difficult—but possible—and important that the organization has its place. Its considerable potential must be judged against these realities.

2. Prospects and Proposals

> . . . man's reach should exceed his grasp . . .
> ROBERT BROWNING, *Andrea del Sarto*

In a sense, the DAC is the keeper of the conscience of the wealthy nations of the free world, reminding them of the lofty goals to which they have set their hand and of their vow to work together toward those goals. But many a Sunday vow is given scant attention during the workday week; and the gap between a resolution of the DAC, the statement of the common aid effort, and the reality of aid policy and of cooperation sometimes seems a chasm.

Yet the resolutions are sincere, if only because the need for cooperative action is so evident. For most of the peoples of the less developed world, the chances for a reasonable standard of achievement are slim enough in any case. Unless the maximum is wrung from the national programs which constitute the bulk of aid, those chances are further diminished. Scarce assets are wasted if the developed nations have no common basis, no consistent methods, and no agreed priorities. The waste is sufficiently clear as to lend urgency to the mutual objectives, the conscientious effort, of the Development Assistance Committee.

Given the nature of bilateral aid, there will be backsliding on the part of members—reluctance to rest decision on the mutual rather than the separate purposes, unwillingness to yield the measure of sovereignty implied in any honestly coordinated endeavor. Yet the DAC can and should be strengthened. Some steps can improve its performance under its present procedures, and some new initiatives can well be taken.

IMPROVEMENTS

The donors have already assigned to the DAC a principal role in the joint analysis of economic aid problems and the construction of a consistent development theory. Several procedural steps might be taken to sharpen the focus of the DAC and to strengthen this role.

1. The Annual Aid Review ought to be reorganized so as to concentrate on what is new, different, or notable in the aid programs of donors. After a few years, formal questioning on policies and procedures which have several times before been described and discussed ceases to have major importance. What is needed is to make the Annual Aid Review sharper, to give it higher selectivity. The increased participation in the review of the chairman and the Secretariat are helpful steps in the right direction.

Some new thought ought to be given to the functions, and consequent organization, of the annual high-level meeting. It could be made more flexible and better designed to adjust to important and current issues, rather than being scheduled by the mandate of the calendar. When developments are meager, the meeting could be attached to the regular annual session of OECD ministers. When, as in 1965, there are matters of importance to be discussed, the meeting ought to be held separately and, again as in 1965, on an unquestionably high level.

2. It would also be useful both to expand the role of the chair-

man in his freedom (with the assistance of the Secretariat) to probe, report, and suggest, and to give authority to the DAC to venture further into the specifics of program coordination. The chairman's report has characteristically been an excellent review and analysis of problems; but, were members to permit, his yearly summation could be made more useful, if he were encouraged to be more incisive and explicit. The chairman could make suggestions to individual members—perhaps in a section of his report reserved to DAC members—on their performance and its betterment. The chairman might be asked to supplement the aid review with a series of visits to capitals for quiet, on-the-spot discussion with officials, putting his findings in the hands of aid administrators, and thus, in a sense, initiating a technical assistance program of sorts among the DAC membership itself.[5]

Such an approach would enhance the value of the analysis of development theory on which the DAC has increasingly been engaged. The early DAC work leading to the Terms of Aid Resolution and the discussion of aid targets have brought about a new sophistication and a new emphasis on the "functional" problems. The heavier emphasis of DAC on this work in cooperation with other international organizations, if done with greater specificity and directness in analysis of the programs of members, could yield interesting discussions and fruitful results. For this achievement, it is probably necessary that chairman and Secretariat be given more independence than they now have.

Exploitation in this way of the resource which is the position

[5] Some steps of this sort have already been taken. Chairman Thorp has visited DAC capitals, and has addressed a commentary on its performance to each of the DAC members, following the aid review. But this kind of practice could well be regularized, the commentary could be sharpened, and there might be profit in combining the Secretariat's analysis of the written presentation prepared for the aid review and the chairman's subsequent comments, and thereafter scheduling "post-mortems" with each donor.

and expertise of the chairman could be supplemented by other methods of bringing the collective experience of the DAC to bear on the policies and programs of individual donors. Conceivably, one might arrive at a kind of consultative group whose deliberations would have an effect on the allocation by DAC members of the totality of their aid. The OECD, in its reviews of the economies of its member countries, does make suggestions which cut deep into national economic policy. It would not be too deep an invasion of the national decision-making process if an organization like the DAC were to take up this same kind of recommendatory power, and were to make suggestions to individual donors designed to improve their programs in the interest of the over-all, and therefore their own, development objectives.

3. If the DAC is to exercise this kind of power, however, it will be necessary for members to take the preliminary decision to strengthen their delegations to it. The United States, with its strong interest in the organization, has had a well-staffed, high-level delegation specially assigned to the DAC and to the developmental side of the OECD. No other delegation is similarly constituted. French representation is unique, the DAC being located where it is. But for other members, and despite frequent attendance by competent officials from capitals, work on the coordination of aid is too often a part-time duty of officials who are general-purpose members of their delegation to the OECD.

The problem here is not the meetings themselves, whether of the DAC or of its working parties. Experts can and do attend those meetings. It is rather the difficulty of establishing a continuing interchange of ideas as well as of information with the objective of improving performance. A related difficulty is also that the representatives are likely to be attuned to the misgivings of finance ministries rather than to the activist policies of aid administrators. This may have something to do with the impression that the program of the DAC for 1965-66 is thus a mere shadow of the strong resolutions adopted at the 1965 high-level meeting.

4. The DAC seems to have abdicated to the World Bank almost all responsibility for consideration of the problems of individual recipients. The tentative steps of the DAC in prior years toward country coordination seem not likely to be followed up. The 1965-66 program contemplates no regional reviews and no country studies, although the problems of particular recipient countries not covered by consortia or consultative groups *may* be the subject of meetings if members consider it useful.

The program for 1965-66 emphasizes the esoteric questions of aid technique—the work of the Expert Group on the Uses of Analytical Techniques. It mentions the problems of fair sharing of the aid burden. It suggests—at this late date!—a special *ad hoc* group to make proposals for a work program on private investment. To examine an individual recipient country in order to see whether the bilateral aid programs are in fact working well or badly, to explore whether they conflict with or complement each other, is apparently terrain which the donors of aid, combined in the DAC, have timidly relinquished.

Yet it is dubious that development theory has much relevance except in the context of the individual, differentiated instance of each developing country. The World Bank has pointed out the dangers of generalizing even from the indisputable statistics of debt-service burdens. Each developing nation is *sui generis.* General principles are real only in context. Averages do not tell an accurate story: the man with one foot on a hot stove and the other in a bucket of ice is not, on the whole, comfortable. DAC conclusions on appropriate levels of aid, or terms of aid, or calculations of aid requirements have different relevance to Brazil and Malawi, Guatemala and Nigeria.

The DAC has unfortunately moved away from its potentially most useful area of work—the country study, or the study of some other appropriate geographic unit. It is in the application of aid practice in the field, not in expert analysis of aid theory, that the immediate conflicts between the bilateral aid programs occur. The DAC should take on the country studies for which its composition fits it. And it should, precisely because it is a political as well as an economic body, take on the difficult cases. If an attempt at harmonization is to mean anything significant, it should be the cases where donors clash, where politics and economics are intertwined, that should occupy the DAC. If this kind of work is not to be done by the DAC, then the organization has no real claim to existence; studies can better be done in universities or in the calm of the OECD Development Center; consortia can better be led by the IBRD.

In an extensive program of country studies there will, of course, be problems with the developing countries themselves. The DAC is, after all, not their club. But it has sufficiently proved its good will to have overcome much of their possibly exaggerated initial reluctance. And in any case a healthy realism will recognize that there is more to gain than to lose from country studies, and that a joining of forces is a likely result.

The most needed procedural reform for the DAC—and one without which it may well fade into innocuous desuetude—is to refocus on coordination where it takes effect, that is, in the recipient nation. Nor is this merely a question of giving useful work to just another international institution. The special characteristics of the DAC—its limited and relatively homogeneous membership, its capacity to handle the political as well as the economic aspects of aid, its mingling of high purpose and self-interest—make it uniquely fitted for the shaping of free-world aid policy toward individual developing countries. If it tries to explore American and French and Japanese and Canadian aid policies toward Indonesia or Tanzania, it may encounter rough sailing. But the voyage will suit the purpose for which the vessel is designed.

INITIATIVES

Could the DAC play a more extensive role? The answer depends not so much on the rather timid present posture of the DAC as on whether there are situations in which aid is given by national entities, where national interests loom large but the problems and purposes are common to all. In such circumstances, if a mutual objective blankets the national programs, an institution like the DAC can be more than useful.

On a number of hypotheses, the role of the DAC could change dramatically. Today the United States dominates the aid programs of Latin America, the Middle East, and South Asia; if that pattern were to be altered, it is possible that the United States would press more vigorously than it now does for country coordination in the DAC. If Soviet aid were to increase sharply, the DAC might take on coordination of Western policy in relation to that aid and to its recipients. The concert of the less developed in UNCTAD may force DAC into a stronger coordinative role.

Beyond such speculation is the existing pressure, at least in the United States, for an increasing multilateralization of aid. Senator J. W. Fulbright has forcefully suggested both that he has wearied of the annual battle in the United States Congress for aid authorizations and funds, and that there might be a "true multilateralization" of aid.[6] He has urged "the kind of multilateralization . . . which will vest in an international agency such as the World Bank full authority to determine, *according to objective economic criteria,* who will receive aid and the amounts, kinds and conditions of aid." His suggestion was that "all development loan funds

[6] See *New York Times Magazine,* March 21, 1965.

now administered by our Agency for International Development be turned over to the World Bank's International Development Association (IDA) to be used for long-term low-interest development lending for programs that cannot be financed by conventional loans."

If there is point to the exposition in the preceding pages of the persisting preference of all major donors for their own administration of the bulk of their aid, the Fulbright proposal, however understandable its origins, however commendable its purposes, is a nonstarter. The motives of donors include, but are not limited to, the disinterested development of the less developed. That no progress—indeed, the contrary—has been made in untying bilateral aid suggests that this proposal for IDA administration of American funds is not likely to win over many congressional votes. And, although the balance of payments situation of the United States is variously assessed, as is the effect of tied aid, a proposal to allow procurement in France or Germany, which has been taboo since 1959, can be expected to evoke no enthusiasm whatever. This has in fact been the reaction to the Fulbright proposal, despite its evident thoughtfulness.

It is nevertheless clear that there is substantial attraction in some kind of internationalization of the aid of the free-world donors. One proposal along these lines, in the early days of the DAC, was for the establishment of a DAC "kitty"—funds to be administered by the donors, but with some DAC power to allocate or to assign priorities.

Another suggestion, made by the author, was that *additional* funds be made available by the present donors to the IBRD (or IDA) on a "line-of-credit" basis. This would mean that IDA could examine development projects, agree to their financing, put them out to free-world competitive bidding, and draw for the financing on the line of credit of the country whose nationals had won the contract. Although the proposal would present some operating problems, they seem easily solvable. And the result would be international administration (of an added *part,* not all) of aid funds, with cash not being required until an order was placed. Given sufficient participation in the scheme, the tying of aid would have few of the economic disadvantages normally associated with that practice.

Variants of either of the above-mentioned suggestions, which would result in a substantial program of aid that would be neither entirely bilateral nor multilateral, can be easily formulated. Whatever the particular formula, it will have merit if it increases levels of aid, maximizes efficiency (and lowers costs to the borrower), and enhances the common purpose of the free world. The DAC could be both a potential source of proposals of this kind and a possible administrator of programs thus proposed. Unhappily, it has taken few initiatives, even in what would seem to be its proper terrain—the coordination of bilateral aid. But the pressure of dissatisfaction with strictly bilateral aid, reflected though it be in different ways, may yet renew the dwindling momentum of the DAC.

The DAC began with a strong American initiative. Whatever may have been the background of that initiative, it gave life to a concept of cooperation among the prosperous nations of the free world for the benefit of the developing nations and their peoples. Now more than before, as the slow rate of progress aggravates discontent, it seems important that this concept be reaffirmed and reinforced. In the success of aid the United States has a larger stake than any other nation. A strong, affirmative move to place emphasis on the principle and the practice of cooperation could be based on the Development Assistance Committee. And such a move is possible. To attain the purposes of the common aid effort it is also strongly desirable.

Postscript

And gladly would he learn, and gladly teach
CHAUCER, *Canterbury Tales*

At the end of the Paris day, the delegates rise, stretch, fold papers, fill briefcases, and hasten back to offices for the inevitable reporting telegrams, prior to the evening round of receptions or dinners. Small groups gather in the corridors, sometimes talking of the day's discussion, making an additional point or hammering one home, hoping to influence a colleague or to explain a point that was intentionally or otherwise not apparent in the meeting. Wishes for a pleasant return to capitals, words in anticipation of meeting at the next session, are exchanged. Another DAC session is over.

It is unlikely that momentous decisions have been taken. Most of the participants in the session will feel some weariness of spirit as of body, some sense that all that has been said that day has been said elsewhere and before and often, and will again be said here and elsewhere in the future. Even when there is measurable accomplishment—agreement on a program, some discernible step toward better cooperation, more effective aid—there will be that sense of anticlimax that sours the achievement which has been too long sought and too long debated. Those who have most pressed for the action just taken are likely to be those most affected by this sense of weariness, of small steps laboriously taken.

Yet the DAC, despite all, is a highly useful organization. It could be much more than it is were members to give it the necessary support. It has already performed important services. It might be encouraged to do more. Whether it will be depends largely on the narrowness or the breadth of the vision of its members.

In at least one respect this group of the rich has done well: it has emphasized not the distinctions between the developed and the less developed but their common interests.

This community of interest has always been clear in the purposes and in the work of the organization. The DAC has been not merely a mechanism for coordination of the programs of donors, for elimination of unnecessary conflicts between them in the sole interest of making sure that more results were produced for each dollar or pound or franc spent. It has kept in mind, as its work has demonstrated, its function as a conscience of the developed nations, always voicing the interest of the less developed nations as well as of its membership.

The origins of the DAC lay in the growing economic strength of the nations whose reconstruction was aided by the United States after World War II, and in the American pressures for burden-sharing in the more difficult task of economic development. Its survival and growing importance as an institution have been based in the evident necessity of reconciling a multiplicity of national aid programs, each rooted in the donor's conception of its own best interest. But its present vitality and its future depend on its ability to perform its tasks of analysis and coordination in the full consciousness of responsibilities owed to those who are not present as to those who are. Perhaps the most important result of its work may be to demonstrate the mutuality of interest, not only among the developed nations which are its members, but between them and the less developed countries of the world.

For some years to come, as this essay began by saying, bilateral aid is likely to be the predominant manner of transferring official resources from the rich to the poor. There are even now many donors; hopefully, in the future there will be more. Given these facts (or assumptions), the DAC, or something like it, becomes not merely useful but necessary. For it is the principal vehicle through which nations with objectives justifying the phrase "the common aid effort" may reconcile their differences, improve their knowledge and their programs, test their theories against practice, and seek to persuade others to their point of view. It is not the World Bank, or a consortium, or a regional lending institution. As the Pope lacks armies, it lacks funds. But it does have some measure of moral authority, a great deal of expertise, and a sound and realistic doctrine. It can do much, for donors and recipients, if it is given the full measure of confidence and support which it merits.

Experience with aid has shown limits on all sides. There are limits to the cooperation which can be expected between donors, between the developing countries themselves, and between the developed and the developing. There are, moreover, limits to the effectiveness of aid in achieving economic development and in promoting social change. Trade policy, population pressures, and other factors are of crucial importance. What will happen in the developing countries is, for the most part, dependent on what political and economic efforts they themselves make. And these are efforts toward a distant goal. To the attainment of that goal, outside aid can give only partial assistance.

It is important that what help foreign aid can give be employed, by donor and recipient alike, as effectively as possible. Despite its failures, its too frequent platitudes, its tendency to attempt little and accomplish less, and, most of all, the limits implicit in the preference of donors for bilateral aid, the DAC has helped to make its members' programs more responsive to the needs of the developing countries. It has illuminated substantive issues: the questions of volume, of distribution, of terms, of the use of technical assistance to make capital assistance effective. It has shown that comparison may be as useful as it is sometimes odious. It has, from time to time, infused discussion of the technicalities of development assistance techniques with verve and excitement.

It is easy, as the 1965 White House Conference on International Cooperation has shown, to urge cooperation for the betterment of mankind—cooperation among the rich, between the developed and the less developed, even between the West and the East. At least one value of the DAC is its capacity, if it is seriously used, to act as a test tube for the first and presumably easiest of these kinds of cooperation—that among the conscientious rich. Its works can be helpful in assaying the realities of the large and hopeful generalities the DAC itself has underlined: that the national interests which inspire the aid programs of the free industrialized countries, and which often conflict on the level of short-range objectives, are, at bottom, harmonious. It can demonstrate that the differences among the Western donors—in emphasis, in historical background, and in specific objectives—are overridden by their common purpose to assist the economic and social progress of that scattered aggregation of nations which, varying in their own stages of growth, in their politics, in their societies, are united in their insistence on their right to rapid development.

The DAC has helped to establish the fact of mutuality between the developed and developing, between donor and recipient. The relationship is fragile, subject to many strains. Resentment, on both sides, lies close beneath its surface. Yet this sometimes tiresome organization in its baroque surroundings, the Development Assistance Committee, has in its curious way underscored the general and mutual interest in effective use of the free world's aid resources. In so doing, this limited group of self-selected nations has taken one step in the difficult journey toward a more lasting and satisfactory world order.

Appendix Table. The Flow of Long-Term Financial Resources to Less Developed

	YEAR	AUS-TRIA	BEL-GIUM	CAN-ADA
TOTAL OFFICIAL AND PRIVATE, NET (I+II+III)	1962	(17.9)	128.4	(96.0)
	1963	(7.9)	171.7	(102.6)
	1964	(15.3)	(136.1)	(149.1)
I. Total official, net	1962	9.1	79.8	54.4
	1963	4.3	89.9	98.0
	1964	13.1	80.0	128.8
A. Total bilateral, net	1962	0.6	64.6	41.9
	1963	2.7	73.4	90.2
	1964	7.3	78.1	111.3
1. Grants and grant-like contributions[1]	1962	0.6	65.6	26.7
	1963	0.7	75.8	51.4
	1964	1.7	76.8	64.2
2. Net lending[2]	1962	—	−1.0	15.2
	1963	2.0	−2.4	38.8
	1964	5.6	1.3	47.1
B. Total multilateral, net	1962	8.5	15.2	12.5
	1963	1.6	16.5	7.8
	1964	5.8	1.9	17.5
of which: Grants to multilateral agencies[3]	1962	1.7	15.2	12.5
	1963	1.6	16.5	12.8
	1964	1.9	1.9	17.5
II. Total private long-term, net	1962	(6.2)	30.8	(41.6)
	1963	(3.6)	57.0	(4.6)
	1964	(1.4)	49.6	(20.3)
of which: Direct investment (including reinvested earnings)	1962	(1.0)	30.0	(30.0)
	1963	(0.8)	50.0	25.0
	1964	(1.0)	50.0	(25.0)
III. Guaranteed private export credits of over 5 years, net	1962	2.6	17.8	—
	1963	—	24.8	—
	1964	0.8	(6.5)	—

Countries and Multilateral Agencies by Major Categories, 1962-1964 (Disbursements)

Million U.S. Dollars

DEN-MARK	FRANCE	GER-MANY	ITALY	JAPAN	NETHER-LANDS	NOR-WAY	PORTU-GAL	UNITED KING-DOM	UNITED STATES	TOTAL DAC COUN-TRIES
13.4	1,286.6	681.5	(281.7)	(302.0)	139.7	(8.4)	—	630.7	4,517	(8,140.5)
(13.9)	1,178.7	557.6	(271.7)	(285.4)	145.2	(24.6)	—	627.4	(4,579)	(8,012.7)
(21.3)	1,288.6	743.6	(159.9)	(277.5)	122.0	(25.6)	—	(799.2)	(4,849)	(8,649.7)
7.4	977.0	427.0	67.0	165.2	90.8	6.8	37.2	417.7	3,713	6,052.4
10.2	843.0	421.5	63.8	171.5	37.8	20.6	47.0	414.2	3,842	6,063.8
11.0	841.4	459.5	56.0	178.4	49.1	17.0	62.8	490.5	3,534	5,921.3
0.7	860.8	324.6	34.9	158.0	46.7	1.2	37.2	377.1	3,440	5,388.3
1.1	813.7	396.2	62.6	159.3	17.9	2.4	47.0	369.5	3,644	5,680.0
2.7	821.8	450.6	61.2	168.9	33.0	2.8	62.7	446.2	3,308	5,554.6
0.8	756.7	109.2	34.5	74.6	42.4	1.3	3.1	211.7	2,697	4,024.2
1.2	678.5	141.4	24.8	76.7	9.9	2.4	8.8	209.1	2,668	3,948.7
3.0	667.7	149.5	20.7	68.7	13.1	2.5	7.5	235.4	2,485	3,795.8
−0.1	104.1	215.4	0.4	83.4	4.3	−0.1	34.1	165.4	743	1,364.1
−0.1	135.2	254.8	37.8	82.6	8.0	—	38.2	160.4	976	1,731.3
−0.3	154.1	301.1	40.5	100.2	19.9	0.3	55.3	210.8	823	1,758.9
6.7	116.2	102.4	32.1	7.2	44.1	5.7	×	40.6	273	664.2
9.1	29.3	25.3	1.2	12.2	19.9	18.2	×	44.7	198	383.8
8.3	19.6	8.9	−5.2	9.5	16.1	14.2	0.1	44.3	226	366.7
6.8	115.2	105.2	19.6	8.7	44.1	6.1	×	40.6	273	648.9
8.1	30.3	30.3	8.9	9.4	18.6	7.5	×	44.7	198	386.7
7.8	16.6	23.9	4.8	9.6	16.1	6.7	0.1	44.3	226	376.9
4.7	295.6	150.1	(186.6)	(103.1)	31.7	(1.6)	..	199.3	769.0	(1,820.3)
(3.0)	297.5	107.4	(129.8)	(100.6)	98.3	(4.0)	..	183.3	(733.0)	(1,722.1)
(2.2)	347.3	194.2	(75.1)	(80.4)	50.2	(5.2)	..	(210.0)	(1,303.0)	(2,338.9)
(3.5)	274.5	92.6	(126.5)	(88.4)	−12.2	(0.8)	..	187.6	564.0	(1,386.7)
(3.0)	280.0	88.9	(102.2)	(96.7)	57.3	(0.4)	..	154.0	714.0	(1,570.0)
(2.2)	334.5	81.0	(60.7)	(59.3)	36.1	(0.7)	..	..	(822.0)	(1,630.0)
1.3	14.0	104.4	(28.1)	33.7	17.2	—	—	13.7	35.0	(267.8)
0.7	38.2	28.7	78.1	13.3	9.1	—	—	29.9	4.0	(226.8)
8.1	99.9	89.9	(28.8)	18.7	22.7	3.4	—	98.7	12.0	(389.5)

Appendix Table. The Flow of Long-Term Financial Resources to Less Developed

	YEAR	AUS-TRIA	BEL-GIUM	CAN-ADA
Memo items:				
1. Official loans for more than 1, up to and including				
5 years, net	1962	4.7	—	—
	1963	−2.2	1.8	—
	1964	2.6	3.4	—
2. Guaranteed private export credits of 1 to 5 years net	1962	7.0	−2.8	5.0
	1963	0.2	7.5	17.9
	1964	4.5	(30.4)	0.8
Memo:				
Totals *including* loans and credits for more than 1, up to and including 5 years' maturity, net[4]				
Total official and private, net	1962	29.6	125.6	(101.0)
	1963	(5.9)	181.0	(120.5)
	1964	(22.4)	169.9	(149.9)
Total official, net	1962	13.8	79.8	54.4
	1963	2.1	91.7	98.0
	1964	15.7	83.4	128.8
Total private, net	1962	15.8	45.8	(46.6)
	1963	(3.8)	89.3	(22.5)
	1964	(6.7)	86.5	(21.1)

[1] Includes loans repayable in recipients' currencies and transfers of resources through sales for recipients' currencies (net of resources realized by donor country by use of these currencies).

[2] Loans exceeding 5 years maturity. Also includes other government bilateral long-term capital.

[3] Includes capital subscription payments.

[4] These totals are shown in order to permit comparison with data and definitions used in the "Flow of Financial Resources to Less-Developed Countries, 1956-1963," and other data based on the IMF definition of "long-term capital."

DEN-MARK	FRANCE	GER-MANY	ITALY	JAPAN	NETHER-LANDS	NOR-WAY	PORTU-GAL	UNITED KING-DOM	UNITED STATES	TOTAL DAC COUN-TRIES
—	—	22.8	42.9	2.9	—	—	3.6	3.3	−42	38.2
−0.5	7.7	2.7	46.4	2.0	—	—	4.1	0.3	−87	−24.7
−0.5	4.4	−43.1	−1.7	32.3	—	—	−0.8	1.5	−75	−76.9
1.1	96.4	−72.3	(84.4)	1.2	0.3	2.4	—	91.7	13.0	(227.4)
−2.7	55.6	28.7	18.7	0.8	−2.8	4.1	—	68.3	26.0	222.3
10.1	67.7	83.7	(78.0)	10.0	−5.0	−0.2	—	37.7	37.0	(354.7)
14.5	1,383.0	632.0	(409.0)	(306.1)	140.0	(10.8)	..	725.7	4,488	(8,406.1)
(10.7)	1,242.0	589.0	(336.8)	(288.2)	142.4	(28.7)	..	696.0	(4,518)	(8,210.3)
(30.9)	1,360.7	784.0	(236.2)	(319.8)	117.0	(25.4)	..	838.4	(4,811)	(8,927.5)
7.4	977.0	449.8	109.9	168.1	90.8	6.8	40.8	421.0	3,671	6,090.6
9.7	850.7	424.2	110.2	173.5	37.8	20.6	51.1	414.5	3,755	6,039.1
10.5	845.8	416.4	54.3	210.7	49.1	17.0	62.0	492.0	3,459	5,844.1
7.1	406.0	182.2	(299.1)	(138.0)	49.2	(4.0)	..	304.7	817	(2,315.5)
(1.0)	391.3	164.8	(226.6)	(114.7)	104.6	(8.1)	..	281.5	(763)	(2,171.2)
(20.4)	514.9	367.8	(181.9)	(109.1)	67.9	(8.4)	..	346.4	(1,352)	(3,083.1)

NOTES: Data in this table are subject to further revision, particularly in respect to the year 1964.

( ) Preliminary figure.

— Nil.

× Less than half the smallest unit shown.

.. Not available.

Slight discrepancies in total are due to rounding.

SOURCE: *Development Assistance Efforts and Policies, 1965 Review,* Report of Willard L. Thorp (Paris: OECD, 1965), pp. 124-125.

Index

COUNCIL ON FOREIGN RELATIONS

Officers and Directors

John J. McCloy, *Chairman of the Board*
Henry M. Wriston, *Honorary President*
Grayson Kirk, *President*
Frank Altschul, *Vice-President & Secretary*
David Rockefeller, *Vice-President*
Gabriel Hauge, *Treasurer*
George S. Franklin, Jr., *Executive Director*

Hamilton Fish Armstrong
Elliott V. Bell
William P. Bundy
William A. M. Burden
Arthur H. Dean
Douglas Dillon
Allen W. Dulles
Thomas K. Finletter
William C. Foster

Caryl P. Haskins
Joseph E. Johnson
Henry R. Labouisse
Walter H. Mallory
James A. Perkins
Philip D. Reed
Whitney H. Shepardson
Charles M. Spofford
Carroll L. Wilson

PUBLICATIONS

FOREIGN AFFAIRS (quarterly), edited by Hamilton Fish Armstrong.

THE UNITED STATES IN WORLD AFFAIRS (annual). Volumes for 1931, 1932 and 1933, by Walter Lippmann and William O. Scroggs; for 1934-1935, 1936, 1937, 1938, 1939 and 1940, by Whitney H. Shepardson and William O. Scroggs; for 1945-1947, 1947-1948 and 1948-1949, by John C. Campbell; for 1949, 1950, 1951, 1952, 1953 and 1954, by Richard P. Stebbins; for 1955, by Hollis W. Barber; for 1956, 1957, 1958, 1959, 1960, 1961, 1962 and 1963, by Richard P. Stebbins; for 1964, by Jules Davids; for 1965, by Richard P. Stebbins.

DOCUMENTS ON AMERICAN FOREIGN RELATIONS (annual). Volume for 1952 edited by Clarence W. Baier and Richard P. Stebbins; for 1953 and 1954, edited by Peter V. Curl; for 1955, 1956, 1957, 1958

162

and 1959, edited by Paul E. Zinner; for 1960, 1961, 1962 and 1963, edited by Richard P. Stebbins; for 1964, edited by Jules Davids; for 1965, edited by Richard P. Stebbins.

POLITICAL HANDBOOK AND ATLAS OF THE WORLD (annual), edited by Walter H. Mallory.

COMMUNIST CHINA'S ECONOMIC GROWTH AND FOREIGN TRADE, by Alexander Eckstein (1966).

TEST BAN AND DISARMAMENT: THE PATH OF NEGOTIATION, by Arthur H. Dean (1966).

THE AMERICAN PEOPLE AND CHINA, by A. T. Steele (1966).

POLICIES TOWARD CHINA: VIEWS FROM SIX CONTINENTS, by A. M. Halpern (1966).

INTERNATIONAL POLITICAL COMMUNICATION, by W. Phillips Davison (1965).

MONETARY REFORM FOR THE WORLD ECONOMY, by Robert V. Roosa (1965).

AFRICAN BATTLELINE: American Policy Choices in Southern Africa, by Waldemar A. Nielsen (1965).

NATO IN TRANSITION: The Future of the Atlantic Alliance, by Timothy W. Stanley (1965).

ALTERNATIVE TO PARTITION: For a Broader Conception of America's Role in Europe, by Zbigniew Brzezinski (1965).

THE TROUBLED PARTNERSHIP: A Re-Appraisal of the Atlantic Alliance, by Henry A. Kissinger (1965).

REMNANTS OF EMPIRE: The United Nations and the End of Colonialism, by David W. Wainhouse (1965).

THE EUROPEAN COMMUNITY AND AMERICAN TRADE: A Study in Atlantic Economics and Policy, by Randall Hinshaw (1964).

THE FOURTH DIMENSION OF FOREIGN POLICY: Educational and Cultural Affairs, by Philip H. Coombs (1964).

AMERICAN AGENCIES INTERESTED IN INTERNATIONAL AFFAIRS (Fifth Edition), compiled by Donald Wasson (1964).

JAPAN AND THE UNITED STATES IN WORLD TRADE, by Warren S. Hunsberger (1964).

FOREIGN AFFAIRS BIBLIOGRAPHY, 1952-1962, by Henry L. Roberts (1964).

THE DOLLAR IN WORLD AFFAIRS: An Essay in International Financial Policy, by Henry G. Aubrey (1964).

ON DEALING WITH THE COMMUNIST WORLD, by George F. Kennan (1964).

FOREIGN AID AND FOREIGN POLICY, by Edward S. Mason (1964).

THE SCIENTIFIC REVOLUTION AND WORLD POLITICS, by Caryl P. Haskins (1964).

AFRICA: A Foreign Affairs Reader, edited by Philip W. Quigg (1964).

THE PHILIPPINES AND THE UNITED STATES: Problems of Partnership, by George E. Taylor (1964).

SOUTHEAST ASIA IN UNITED STATES POLICY, by Russell H. Fifield (1963).

UNESCO: ASSESSMENT AND PROMISE, by George N. Shuster (1963).

THE PEACEFUL ATOM IN FOREIGN POLICY, by Arnold Kramish (1963).

THE ARABS AND THE WORLD: Nasser's Arab Nationalist Policy, by Charles D. Cremeans (1963).

TOWARD AN ATLANTIC COMMUNITY, by Christian A. Herter (1963).

THE SOVIET UNION, 1922-1962: A Foreign Affairs Reader, edited by Philip E. Mosely (1963).

THE POLITICS OF FOREIGN AID: American Experience in Southeast Asia, by John D. Montgomery (1962).

SPEARHEADS OF DEMOCRACY: Labor in the Developing Countries, by George C. Lodge (1962).

LATIN AMERICA: Diplomacy and Reality, by Adolf A. Berle (1962).

THE ORGANIZATION OF AMERICAN STATES AND THE HEMISPHERE CRISIS, by John C. Dreier (1962).

THE UNITED NATIONS: Structure for Peace, by Ernest A. Gross (1962).

THE LONG POLAR WATCH: Canada and the Defense of North America, by Melvin Conant (1962).

ARMS AND POLITICS IN LATIN AMERICA (Revised Edition), by Edwin Lieuwen (1961).

THE FUTURE OF UNDERDEVELOPED COUNTRIES: Political Implications of Economic Development (Revised Edition), by Eugene Staley (1961).

SPAIN AND DEFENSE OF THE WEST: Ally and Liability, by Arthur P. Whitaker (1961).

SOCIAL CHANGE IN LATIN AMERICA TODAY: Its Implications for United States Policy, by Richard N. Adams, John P. Gillin, Allan R. Holmberg, Oscar Lewis, Richard W. Patch, and Charles W. Wagley (1961).